Klondikes, Chipped Ham, & Skyscraper Cones

Brian Butko

To Aunt Florence
from Dick & Barb
10/5/01

Klondikes, Chipped Ham, & Skyscraper Cones

THE STORY OF ISALY'S

Brian Butko

STACKPOLE
BOOKS

Copyright ©2001 by Stackpole Books

Published by
STACKPOLE BOOKS
5067 Ritter Road
Mechanicsburg, PA 17055
www.stackpolebooks.com

Printed in the United States of America

10 9 8 7 6 5 4 3 2

FIRST EDITION

INTERIOR DESIGN BY BETH OBERHOLTZER
LAYOUT BY KERRY JEAN HANDEL
COVER DESIGN BY CAROLINE STOVER
COVER ILLUSTRATIONS FROM AUTHOR'S COLLECTION
FRONTISPIECE COURTESY WILLIAM R. ISALY

Library of Congress Cataloging-in-Publication Data

Butko, Brian A.
    Klondikes, chipped ham & skyscraper cones : the story of Isaly's / Brian Butko.
    —1st ed.
        p.   cm.
    ISBN 0–8117–2844–7
    1. Isaly's (Firm)–History.   2. Dairy products industry–United States–History.
3. Ice cream industry–United States–History.   4. Convenience stores–United States–History.   5. Chain stores–United States–History.   6. Dairy products industry–Ohio–History.   7. Dairy products industry–Pennsylvania–History.   I. Title.

HD9275.U8 I833   2001
338.7′6371′0973–dc21

                                                                                    00–068765

CONTENTS

FOREWORD

*W*HEN I WAS GROWING UP IN THE 1950s IN GREENVILLE, PENNSYLVANIA, Isaly's was the premier destination for ice cream—hard ice cream, that is. The local Isaly's store, with its shiny white Vitrolite front, occupied the ground floor of a narrow brick building in the lively Main Street business district, close to everything in the heart of town. Those were my elementary school years, and I had the illusion that Isaly's, like most good things, was eternal.

At the start of each morning, downtown workers in need of an early cup of coffee would fill wooden booths along the wall or low stools at a counter, while light from the hanging fixtures reflected off the pressed tin ceiling. At lunchtime, people gathered for sandwiches, chili, meat loaf, and other homestyle fare, served from the steam table at the back of the store. Employees at the deli counter sliced wafer-thin chipped chopped ham that Isaly's had made a regional favorite. In the afternoon, when captive adolescents were released from the high school, they would rush in for Skyscraper cones and Klondike bars.

The same scene was played out in hundreds of Isaly's across the region. But eventually I realized that Isaly's was not eternal after all. A fierce competition was waged in the fifties: Hard ice cream was challenged by soft-serve concoctions like the semi-frozen dessert that Dairy Queen had developed. Traditional business districts—congested blocks with a shortage of parking spaces—began to lose trade to drive-ins and automobile-convenient shopping centers on cheaper outlying land. In time, the Isaly's stores vanished.

Fortunately, Brian Butko has come along to research the Isaly's story and present it in wonderful detail in this welcome book. Butko has gotten to know the people, products, atmosphere, and management techniques that made Isaly's stand out during its heyday. His words should leave no doubt as to why the mention of Isaly's still arouses a lingering pleasure, tempered by a wistful sense that yet another good thing has disappeared.

Philip Langdon

PHILIP LANGDON IS AUTHOR OF *ORANGE ROOFS, GOLDEN ARCHES: THE ARCHITECTURE OF AMERICAN CHAIN RESTAURANTS* AND *A BETTER PLACE TO LIVE: RESHAPING THE AMERICAN SUBURB.*

PREFACE

*T*HE **KLONDIKE WAS NOT THE FIRST CHOCOLATE-COATED ICE CREAM BAR,** and for 60 years, it was sold only around Pittsburgh and in Ohio. Yet since 1996, Klondike has been America's best-selling ice cream novelty. Its recent quick rise is remarkable, but only part of the roller-coaster saga of the company that created it, Isaly's.

Isaly's (EYES-leez) was named for the Isaly family. Their chain grew to 11 plants and more than 400 dairy stores, but even though most are now closed, people speak of them with a reverence bordering on fanaticism. Over and over I've heard, "Their ice cream was the best." Or their potato salad. Or cottage cheese. Or baked beans. Over and over I've heard how wonderful it was to work for Isaly's, how it was like a big family. All this unabashed admiration set me on a mission to find out what created so much goodwill.

I interviewed and corresponded with more than 200 customers, workers, and family. I dug through articles, sales reports, and incorporation papers (I stopped counting these at 600). And it became obvious: People loved Isaly's because, from the top down, Isaly's cared. The Isalys cared about the quality of their products. They bought the most innovative equipment. They cared about the cleanliness of their stores and how merchandise was displayed. And they especially cared for people, both patrons and employees. This benevolence permeated the company and has now outlasted most of the stores. The people you'll meet in this story say it best:

- I knew every manager, every assistant manager, and I knew their families, I knew how many kids they had, and in those days, if we had a manager who maybe had a child that was having trouble, we helped, without making a lot of noise about it. We helped financially, and we did things for them.
- People trusted us. We didn't put in garbage, make no mistake, we never took any garbage, we never took any junk. If it wasn't good, we didn't have it.
- We were hard taskmasters. We had an image and we wanted that image to stay as pristine as we knew how to make it.
- They wanted a customer to be satisfied from the time they walked in to the time they left that store, and they wanted them back. I never heard "cut this and cut corners." They wanted a good bottom line, but they didn't want it that way.

- The one thing about Isaly's was they taught you how to make money and how to care for people. . . . I always looked forward to unlocking that front door.
- God bless Isaly, whoever he was.

It goes on and on, which is why it's all the more mysterious that those beloved Isaly's stores are all but gone. Why did they disappear? That was the rest of my mission.

• • •

Here are some of the key players who help tell the Isaly's story:

- George Krohe: rose from Pittsburgh scooper in 1931 to vice-president—the company's "heart"
- Claire "Larry" Hatch: manager who whipped Pittsburgh stores into shape starting in the 1930s
- Art Frank: another scooper who rose to vice-president, but in Youngstown
- H. William Isaly: president in the 1960s; managed Klondike plant until the 1990s
- Gaylord LaMond: bought the company from the Isaly family in the 1970s
- Henry Clarke: took the Klondike national in the 1980s

• • •

I'm grateful to the Isaly family for letting a stranger enter their lives and dissect a century of personal and business dealings. I wish I could have included more of the hundreds of wonderful stories and photos that family members, workers, and customers sent. I had help from many friends, especially Bill Andrews, who shared his research, and Rick Sebak, who offered access to his "Things" interviews both in print and for the exhibit video. Just about all my fellow employees at the Historical Society of Western Pennsylvania assisted, as did hundreds of librarians, archivists, and town historians. As always, big thanks go to my wife, Sarah Butko, and to Stackpole editor Kyle Weaver. And finally, thanks to George Krohe, who, more than anyone, helped me with this book.

Klondikes, Chipped Ham, & Skyscraper Cones

Swiss Dairymen

YES, ISALY'S MANUFACTURED DAIRY PRODUCTS AND SOLD THEM IN ITS CHAIN OF stores, but George Krohe (KRO-ee) would set you straight: "Isaly's was more than just a company or a job. It was a way of life."

Krohe joined Isaly's in 1931, a week after the company opened a plant in Pittsburgh. He'd been making good money as a civil engineer with the Union Railroad when the depression threw him out of work, so the 21-year-old tried Isaly's new plant on the Boulevard of the Allies. General manager and treasurer Henry Isaly, himself just 25, said they had no openings, but Krohe persisted:

> Mr. Isaly showed me the delicatessen counter, and I said, "Well, I have experience in that, I can sell meat and cheese."
>
> "Well then, we have this lunch counter."
>
> And I said, "Oh, that's easy, 'cause I worked in a drugstore." I was givin' him a sales job. It was true, but it was a sales job.
>
> He said, "You couldn't make those ice cream cones."
>
> I said, "Will you let me try?"
>
> "I'll tell you what, you come back at one o'clock and you can start."
>
> This is ten o'clock in the morning, so I said, "I'll work for nothing from now until one, so I'll be here." A job was hard to find.
>
> He said, "No, you come back at one o'clock, you'll have a job."
>
> The first week I worked night and day, and I ended up making $13.75 at 25 cents an hour. But that was all right.

Krohe became a clerk, a position of respect because of the skill required to make the company's Skyscraper cones. The tall cones were but one of Isaly's draws; as Krohe explained, Isaly's "was the first thing in the depression years where somebody was giving you something better than your money's worth."

Detail of a Swiss dairy scene that hung in Isaly's stores.
GAYLORD LaMOND

So how did Isaly's give such value? How did the company have the audacity to enter Pittsburgh and build a four-story plant in the depths of the depression? George Krohe answers that by recalling a time years later when he approached Henry Isaly about changing a product to save the company money. Henry's response: "Let's give the profits to the customers, not the stockholders."

Many in the Isaly family had the same generous tendencies, along with a knack for innovation, efficiency, and hard work. The family proudly attributes some of this to their Swiss heritage. First to leave Switzerland for America was Christian Iseli. In 1833, Christian brought his young family and their copper cheese kettle to Switzer Township, Ohio. It looked like the land they had left: too hilly for plowing, but perfect for pasture. By 1881, 20-year-old grandson William was running a dairy farm and managing a cheese factory.

Some farmers found the area too mountainous and left. In 1892, William moved 100 miles to Mansfield, Ohio. When he found the pasture there not so good for making Swiss cheese, William turned to selling his milk by wagon (or sled) to hotels and restaurants. But he could only sell locally; pasteurization, which delays spoilage by partially sterilizing milk with heat, was just becoming practical.

In 1902, William and friends bought a milk plant and 26 routes to form the Mansfield Pure Milk Company (use of the word "pure" was a common way to assure consumers the milk was pasteurized or unadulterated). They incorporated in 1904 with 100 shares of $100 stock ($10,000–almost $200,000 in today's money). William, the president and manager, convinced his cousin Jesse back in Switzer Township to join him. William had Americanized his name to Isaly; Jesse changed his name too, moved to Mansfield, and became treasurer of the new corporation.

George Krohe at the Homewood Isaly's, east of Pittsburgh, in 1932. From left: Helen Hartley, Jim Wilson, Krohe, and Sue Phieffer. GEORGE KROHE

Christian and Verena Iseli's home lies abandoned in Switzer Township, Ohio, named for its numerous Swiss settlers. PHOTO BY THE AUTHOR

In 1909, Mansfield Pure Milk purchased the Loiselle Bread and Milk Company and moved into its plant. A small store was set up inside to sell milk, butter, and ice cream: vanilla, chocolate, strawberry, and maple.

The ice cream cone, just five years old, was not yet a big draw, so William Isaly increased his 5¢ cones from the typical two ounces to four, and business boomed: Records show 7,600 cones scooped one day in 1912. One tale claimed that a stranger saw the crowd and asked the corner policeman, "Did someone get shot?"

"Yes, Isaly's shooting them with ice cream cones."

William Isaly made his first leap to new territory in 1914 by purchasing the Marion Pure Milk Company, 35 miles to the west. William was again president, but his 26-year-old son Charles was made manager and treasurer. Charles's wife Bertie later recalled her role as spouse of an "executive": milking cows, washing 40 milk cans daily, selling cones at the plant, and driving a milk route that included bookkeeping and delivering fish in a wagon drawn by horses—and sometimes mules!

Charles's business card "explained" what each of the letters in "Isaly's" stood for, with gems such as "S Stands for Safe Milk that Merits Your Trade," and "L Stands for Luciousness [*sic*] and Laudible [*sic*] Flavor." Most prominent on the card was Isaly's creamery butter, a nod to its factory origins as opposed to farm churning.

It was essential that the Marion purchase include a dairy plant, as primitive roads and

The famous copper cheese kettle was displayed for years at various Isaly's plants. WILLIAM R. ISALY

The Mansfield Pure Milk Company bought this plant on North Franklin Street in 1909.
MARGARET ISALY HERRMANN

Barrels packed with salt and ice hold ice cream sold from this office in the Mansfield plant.
A customer, left, is greeted by Isaly relative Fred Luedy, Mr. Campbell, Edith (House) Wilcox,
and Samuel Isaly, scooping a cone from the open lid. SAMUEL D. ISALY

trucks necessitated a separate factory. The Marion branch was incorporated as The Isaly Dairy Company; Charles's son John Isaly recalled that "the shareholders of one company weren't necessarily the same as another company, let alone being in the same proportion." This arrangement—so necessary at the time—would return to haunt the company.

Within two years, Marion had grown from 4 to 14 routes. Plowing profits back into expansion, Isaly's opened a third branch in 1918 by purchasing the plant and routes of Farmer's Dairy in Youngstown, a booming steel town 100 miles east of Mansfield. The property at 1033 Mahoning Avenue offered room to finally build a dairy from scratch. The lot came with two houses: One was knocked down to build the new plant, and the other became home for William's 31-year-old son Chester, who was made manager and treasurer. With him came wife Nelle and young daughters Margaret and Helen.

Chester was recalled in a period article as "a rugged, but gentle-dispositioned man, with Swiss staunchness." Margaret remembered, "Our father got up very, very early and went to work. We never saw him because he had to check out the cottage cheese." Helen added: "He had to have his hand in everything except the purse strings and the office, and that was my mother's. . . . She did all the billing, she knew all the drivers by name, she was the driving force and the money watcher. . . . Margaret and I were her children, but her baby was the dairy."

The Isaly family about 1917. Top row: Samuel, Chester's wife Nelle, Chester, Selma, Selma's husband John Mahon, and Josephine. Middle row: Henry, William, William's wife Louisa (Luedy), Charles's wife Bertie, and Charles. The small children are Charles and Bertie's: Richard, Marian, and baby William R. MARGARET ISALY HERRMANN

I Shall Always Love You

Market penetration was so strong that many remember signing letters and love notes, "I-S-A-L-Y," for "I Shall Always Love You." Some even added the final "S" for "Sweetheart."

Isaly's

ENDS THE QUEST FOR THE BEST

Within a few months, Youngstown's paper called Isaly's "one of the leading distributors of the city." Isaly's had surprised established dealers by reducing milk from 14¢ to 12¢ a quart; Chester said the secret to cutting costs was to systemize distribution, then build volume. By 1921, the plant employed 40, operated 6 trucks and 10 wagons, and was adding a three-story garage.

The Mansfield Pure Milk branch was also prospering; in 1920, its capital stock was increased from $15,000 to $200,000, and its name was officially changed to The Isaly Dairy Company of Mansfield, Ohio. William's son Samuel was made treasurer (Jesse switched to superintendent), while William concentrated on building a certified dairy farm to produce nonpasteurized milk for babies. His sons now held prominent positions at all three branches, but instead of sitting still, they took his concepts and revolutionized the company.

· · ·

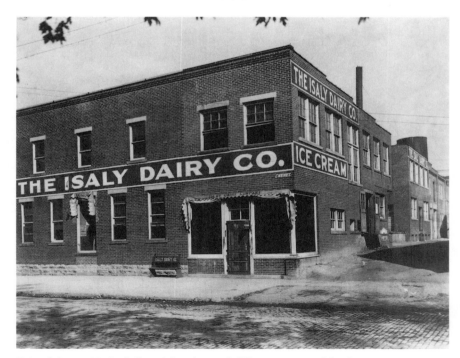

Painted signs at Marion indicated that the rear buildings were part of the plant. WILLIAM R. ISALY

A gas station and garage sat behind the Youngstown plant. Note the garage-top ad for the company's Cloverleaf butter. The globes atop the pumps advertise "Vahey Products," and the tank truck next to the station reads "The Vahey Oil Co., Marwood Gasoline, IDOIL." The business was incorporated in 1934 as the Idee Oil Co. (Idee/ID stood for Isaly's Dairy), and the logo resembled the Isaly family crest. MARGARET ISALY HERRMANN

Except for the tiny stand in the Mansfield plant, Isaly's products were all sold on delivery routes, incurring costs for delivery and icing. Home delivery was a credit risk, and as for retail, William and sons couldn't convince storekeepers to clean up their stores, let alone merchandise products. As an industry journal later explained, the Isalys "watched customers buy ice cream and heard them grumble at the 1½-ounce nickel cone and 2½- to 3-ounce dime dishes. They knew the ice cream parlor's long mark-up, but they were unable to teach the proprietors the value of narrow margins with greater gross profits through volume sales."

William hit upon the idea of expanding his in-plant stand to open his own dairy stores where there were no middlemen, only cash-paying customers. The idea was tried initially with franchises: The first Youngstown franchise opened on Central Square in 1918, and six years later, there were 25 stores around town. The first wholly company-owned store opened in 1921 in Mansfield, managed by William's son-in-law John Mahon (husband of Selma).

A key advantage of direct-to-consumer sales was that bigger profits could be made without undercutting competition. A 1924 industry publication proclaimed, "The 'Isaly idea' has long been the cynosure of all eyes in the dairy industry. . . . [P]roducts were priced the same as those sold by other concerns. The stores, therefore, have interfered little with [others'] milk delivery business or the retail grocery trade. In fact, they have helped increase milk and ice cream consumption, to the benefit of all engaged in the dairy business."

William Isaly, the article explained, "believed . . . that people will buy where they get more for their money." He taught his sons "to know their customers through personal contact in retail stores. . . . Look for an Isaly behind the counter—he'll be there because customers like it and the Isalys learn from their customers."

Klondike 1922

Charles summed up their formula for success: uniform quality, courteous and prompt service, cleanliness, and "being willing to share your profits with your customers . . . making it worth their while to walk or drive a few blocks for a quart of ice cream or a couple of cones."

Their success indeed stemmed from those big cones pioneered by William: "Isaly reasoned that if the ice cream volume through its own outlets could be stepped up to some eight or ten times the volume of the average drug store, the saving in delivery costs would be quite considerable." Cones also didn't require "dishes, silver, tables, chairs, waitresses, washers, and floor space." And high turnover meant fresher ice cream.

Cones were a tough sell at first, as they were seen as a child's treat, but the 1924 article said that each Isaly's grand opening "thaws out all inhibitions. Free cones are given away as fast as they can be scooped out." Up to 20,000 cones were given away at store openings, twice that at plant openings. Though farmers received a lower rate for milk classified for ice cream, Isaly's used its savings to pay farmers a 15 percent premium, making friends in that corner too.

And long before colleges offered courses on consumer habits, Isaly's put its ice cream counters in back. With 60 percent of sales occurring there, "Many an impulse sale of cheese, cold cuts or delicatessen results from the purchase of an ice cream cone. . . . Isaly neither locates nor operates by guess."

Success brought more Isaly relatives into the business. William Isaly's daughter Josephine and her husband John Bricker moved to Sharon, Pennsylvania, in 1924 to open the first of five Isaly's for them. Bricker's brothers Lee, Tommy, and Harry also opened stores. Lee hesitated leaving his farm—he was a 43-year-old family man—but in 1930, he gathered $250 to open an Isaly's in East Liverpool, Ohio. To accommodate the late shift of the region's potteries, Lee operated from 6 A.M. to 2 A.M. His son Harold Bricker remembered, "In the summer, it was hard for us to get the store closed because of the number of people downtown at that time of night." The store is still there (as is nearby Homer Laughlin Company, maker of Fiesta ware), but it's been called Bricker's for years, and it closes a lot earlier.

Harry Bricker's son Dean recalled tweaking Isaly's profits-from-volume policy at the Beaver Falls, Pennsylvania, franchise: "They were too close-margin for us. For instance, Isaly butter carried 1¢ profit on it, and you'd go through that by the ton on a Saturday and not make any money, so we always asked for a nickel."

As Isaly's expanded, it hatched another enticement: the Klondike ice cream bar. The name was a nod to the Klondike Gold Rush of the 1890s, spurred by the discovery of gold in a tributary of the Klondike River in Canada's Yukon Territory.

The earliest mention of Klondike is a February 5, 1922, article in the *Youngstown Vindicator* saying that Chester had given the staff several dozen bars in strawberry, vanilla, chocolate, grape, maple, and cherry—each coated in chocolate. The same day's paper had numerous ads straining to associate with the film premier of *Little Lord Fauntleroy*, starring Mary Pickford. Isaly's joined the fray by advertising that "Little Lord Fauntleroy liked chocolate nut sundaes. If he was in Youngstown he would certainly eat Klondikes, 10¢ each." The six flavors could be found at Isaly Dairy Stations plus the Hotel Union Grill and Donahoe's Inc.

At this early Youngstown Isaly's, more than $180,000 worth of dairy products was reportedly sold here in one year, and in 1923, over 42,000 gallons of ice cream were sold. Isaly's Cloverleaf butter can be seen stacked behind the register, far right. MARGARET ISALY HERRMANN

The stores were mini versions of the plant store; in fact, the first Mansfield store at Fourth and Mulberry Streets was always called the Sub Station. The opening ad advertised, "Milk, cream, Goldenspread butter, ice cream, buttermilk, and our big ice cream cones will be sold at the same prices as at our plant." MARGARET ISALY HERRMANN

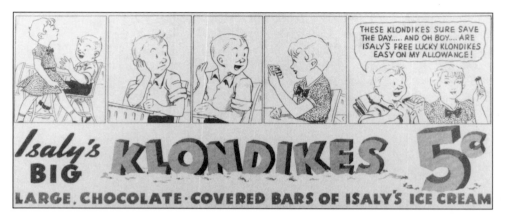

This ad highlights the "lucky coupons" that entitled the bearer to a free Klondike—in this case, to share. AUTHOR'S COLLECTION

"Our understanding of the Klondike," said Chester's daughter Margaret, "was the Eskimo Pie had come out and our father had said if it's just ice cream with a chocolate cover, well we can do the same." Another scenario of the Klondike's origin, however, was adhered to by Sam Isaly, son of Chester's brother Samuel: "Legend around me, including that from my mother and from my cousin, Walter Paulo, was that my father came up with the formulation in his kitchen or his parents' kitchen." Indeed, company press releases long told of Sam concocting the bars at home, but that version claimed he started in 1929.

Marian Isaly Schulz also believes her father, Charles, helped develop the bar: "I know Dad had a part in naming it. There were several names put up, and Dad had suggested Klondike. . . . Klondike was pretty good, one word and visual, and you feel cold to think about it." But she doesn't press the issue: "It's too much of a family thing to make it a sore point."

In fact, Marion, Ohio, resident Robert Hinklin said *his* dad, Marion Hinklin, gave the name to Charles: "Seems as how old Charlie Isaly was walking through the plant, grumbling about the competition having created the Eskimo Pie, and Dad then offered that Isaly's should counter by calling their product the Klondike." However, Hinklin said his dad worked in the shipping department from 1924 to 1936, after the Klondike was invented. But adding to the mystery is a 1922 photo showing Hinklin on Isaly's basketball team.

Wilbur & Sons chocolate company was also then advertising a near-identical name for its ice cream bar coatings. An ad in the March 1922 *Ice Cream Review* pictured a giant bar surrounded by Eskimos, with Klondike Chocolate and Klondike Star Chocolate among the firm's five coatings.

Most likely, each of the brothers (and spouses and employees) made a suggestion here or an improvement there. Besides, Eskimo Pie had already swept the dairy industry by storm in 1921. More revealing, Good Humor debuted soon after that *in Youngstown.* The above-mentioned 1922 Klondike ad ran just six days after Good Humor inventor Harry Burt filed patent applications for an

"Ice Cream Sucker" and an "Apparatus For Making Frozen Confections," and it's been rumored that Burt and the Isalys helped each other. Good Humors were on a stick—like Youngstown-made Klondikes—and had "lucky sticks" like Klondike's lucky sticks, cards, and pink centers, which awarded the recipient a free bar. The pink centers left an especially big impression, as customer Jean Moon affirms: "I'm not sure if I ever 'won' a free bar, but the anticipation of such a thing happening was so great that I feel that I won just from thinking about it."

Ice cream packaging machines were appearing, but equipment to reliably automate novelties like the Klondike came much later. Machinery had been invented, however, to make bars on a stick like Good Humor because the stick could be used for dipping. Isaly's Youngstown management embraced the cost-saving technology and made its Klondikes with sticks.

But George Krohe said of the youngest brother, "Henry Isaly always said that Klondike is an adult bar. He would never put a stick in it." So Isaly's other plants continued making stickless Klondikes that were cut and dipped by hand. Charles's son William R. Isaly helped bag Klondikes in the 1920s: "The big cutter would cut the slabs into Klondike-size ice cream bars, and this fellow would have these hooks. He'd take one out and put the hook in and dip it [in a kettle of chocolate], hang it on [a rod], and he'd go all the way around. By that time, this would be dry and he'd bang it off onto a box." The bars were more often made by "Klondike girls," the lone job at the plants for women (other than Isaly family members).

Despite the human touch, Klondikes were vastly more sanitary than ice cream made and sold by street vendors. The era saw important advances in

Klondikes were originally sold in glassine bags. WILLIAM R. ISALY

Novelties

After the success of Eskimo Pie starting in 1921, every manufacturer tried to get in on the fad. A look through a 1922 trade magazine found 25 ads for ice cream bar products, plus news features and an editorial, "Is the Chocolate Covered Ice Cream Bar Here to Stay?" A decade later, a survey of 130 ice cream

makers found 297 novelties representing 93 different kinds. Most manufacturers admitted that novelties were unprofitable, but they had to meet the competition.

Sources: Ice Cream Review, March 1922; W. H. List Jr., "Novelties," *Abstracts of Literature on the Manufacture and Distribution of Ice Cream* (Harrisburg, PA: Intl. Assn. of Ice Cream Mfrs., 1933).

refrigeration, homogenization, and transport, though most ice cream was still stored in wet, salty packing tubs, discouraging home use. Refrigerators were selling for almost $1,000 at a time when few homes were even wired for electricity. Ice cream was a special treat, and except for a few do-it-yourselfers, those who wanted it had to go buy it and carry it home.

But life was changing. In 1920, Americans owned 20,000 electric refrigerators; by 1930, they had 850,000 and the cost had dropped below $100. Inventions like porcelainized steel simplified cleaning, while wax cartons made keeping foods easier. As refrigerator ownership increased, so did sales of bulk ice cream: Products like Isaly's quart-sized "bricks" were tailored for the tiny freezer compartments.

All this contributed to soaring ice cream sales: 5 million gallons were produced nationally in 1899; 95 million gallons in 1910; 257 million gallons in 1920; and 465 million gallons in 1929. Prohibition left bankrupt breweries turning to ice cream production to satisfy drinkers looking for something to fill the void. Chocolate-coated bars became so popular that in the late 1920s, the U.S. Department of Commerce reported novelties' demand for cocoa brought about a recovery in economically depressed Ecuador.

William Isaly didn't get to see much of the boom: He passed away in 1923. Son Samuel assumed presidency of Mansfield, Marion, and Youngstown, while Chester continued managing the Youngstown plant, as did Charles in Marion. The three brothers now oversaw more than 40 stores.

At the 1926 annual meeting, Chester announced that the public could soon tour the company's 250-acre dairy farm his dad had started near Youngstown, where raw milk from 50 tuberculin-tested Holsteins was marketed for babies. As a 1927 article explained, the barn even had concrete floors and steam heat so as to assure "milk from contented cows." Chester also announced that a 20 percent increase in business that year required enlarging the Youngstown plant (and thereby demolishing his house).

In fact, Isaly's was prospering enough that at the 1929 annual meeting, stockholders were presented with a merger proposal by a national company, surely National Dairy Products. Isaly's, however, had just finished its best year ever—the company could now sell its entire plant output through its own stores—so it had no need for mergers. In fact, plans were under way to challenge National Dairy on its home turf.

• • •

Henry Isaly was the baby of the William Isaly family, only 24 years old when the company expanded again in 1929. He'd graduated from Cornell with a degree in dairy technology and had already managed the Mansfield branch. Henry was tall and husky and had a personality that made him very popular. Longtime employee George Krohe remembered "he had a twinkle in his eye." Like his brothers, Henry is remembered fondly, even decades after his death.

Although Isaly's hadn't penetrated all of Ohio, the company's next move was to Pittsburgh. Dairy-intensive Ohio had many restrictive milk regulations, so young Henry didn't mind the risk of entering a different state. Charles's son John Isaly said Henry played a key role: "Henry looked at the demographics as he could see them in that day and age [and decided] that Pittsburgh probably fit in with what we were doing, maybe better than the Cleveland demographics." Pittsburgh indeed was more like a gathering of small towns rather than one big one, with distinct neighborhoods anchored to each hill and hollow.

A four-acre plot was chosen on the Boulevard of the Allies. Its Oakland neighborhood was home to the University of Pittsburgh, Carnegie Institute of Technology (now Carnegie Mellon University), and Forbes Field, ballpark for the Pirates and—after 1933—the Steelers.

Henry Isaly was made manager and treasurer of the new company, his brother Charles president, and Samuel secretary. Vice-presidency went to John Martig, the "cheese king of America" and Isaly's biggest stockholder. Martig had immigrated from Switzerland in 1893 at age 16, and by the time he was 35, he controlled 80 cheese factories, yet he and his wife never hired any salesmen or helpers for the warehouse or the office. Chester's daughter Helen said it was Martig who financed the building of Isaly's Youngstown plant. He had retired in the 1920s, a millionaire.

Milk Innovations Help Ice Cream

A number of innovations in the processing of milk led to the popularization of ice cream. In 1856, Gail Borden was granted a patent for condensed milk, which became a popular ingredient to give ice cream more body. (Solids without the fat could be extracted and stored until needed.) The homogenizer, invented in France in 1899, meant that ice cream was no longer tied to the availability of fresh cream, which was highly perishable. Most of all, mechanical refrigeration eased all aspects of ice cream production: the transport of milk, the manufacture of ice cream, its storage, and its delivery.

Source: K. A. Hyde and J. Rothwell, *Ice Cream* (Edinburgh: Churchill Livingstone, 1973).

The Boulevard plant became an integral part of the Oakland community east of Pittsburgh, where J & L Steel lined the river. George Krohe said that most plant employees were from the neighborhood, "and almost every one of these boys worked as an usher, a ticket taker, or something at Forbes Field." Baseball fans flooded the Boulevard after a Pirates game. Customers marveled at the long deli case, many of them learning about "take-out" food for the first time. The Boulevard, in fact, took on mythic status, as customers chainwide could soon buy "Boulevard" brand coffee, eggs, potato chips, and more. The white plant shines in the distance while the Pirates play the Dodgers, July 6, 1953. CARNEGIE LIBRARY, PITTSBURGH

George Krohe also heard about Martig's effect on Isaly's and its stockholders: "They were a bunch of farmers, and they acted like farmers. They came to Pittsburgh and they looked at the lot that they had on the Boulevard of the Allies, and they had their meeting. You think they had it at the William Penn or one of the big hotels? No, they went up into Schenley Park and pulled tables together and they had their first meeting there. This was an unknown thing at the time, and they were all bidding, 'Let's see, I'll take 10 shares of stock' . . . and they came to John Martig—he was about three-quarters of the way down the line—and they said, 'John, what will you take?' He said, 'I won't take any now, but you sell all the rest, and what's left over, I'll buy everything.' Boy, they all got on the bandwagon."

Henry Isaly moved to Pittsburgh and got a job—at the delicatessen in Donahoe's popular downtown market. "He wanted to learn the people of Pittsburgh," said Krohe.

The stock market crashed a month after the Pittsburgh branch was incorporated, but Isaly's pressed forward, despite the looming depression: "'capital and courage' brought about the greatest expansion," one article said. "Management knew that whatever economic conditions might be, people would always drink milk."

The Boulevard (as the plant was called) was designed by dairy and bakery architect William D. McCormick. The 100-foot-square plant was glazed brick inside with an art deco exterior of white, cream, tan, and black terra cotta. Zoning forced it back from the road, but this became an asset, allowing the building's beauty to be better seen, plus cars could pull right up to the ground-floor salesroom. Construction, though, was delayed a year when nearby Magee Hospital protested that there would be early-morning noise from the loading of trucks. Magee relented, and later, Isaly's even stored its milk, but Pittsburgh's first six stores were serviced from Youngstown until the plant was at full capacity.

The Boulevard land, building, and equipment cost more than half a million dollars ($5 million today), not including trucks or inventory. Isaly's invested heavily, despite having no market presence and only its *planned* stores as outlets. And Isaly's was doing all this in, as one article described it, "an ultra-conservative Eastern city where the milk and ice cream companies were well and long established." Leading the pack was Rieck-McJunkin, a huge regional company that in 1923 had formed the basis of National Dairy; by 1925, National operated 31 plants in 23 cities; by 1929, it had acquired Breyer's Ice Cream and Kraft and would later popularize Sealtest.

Such worries weighed heavy on oldest brother Chester. Late in 1930, he began suffering from a nervous disorder that affected his heart; Youngstown employees found him on the roof three times in one day. Finally, he and wife Nelle went to their St. Petersburg, Florida, home to rest for six weeks. They returned in March 1931, and Chester seemed in good spirits. One morning, he drove Nelle downtown and returned to the plant as usual. But just after 9 A.M., a shot rang from a third-floor washroom; at age 44, Chester Isaly was dead. Company officials reported that he'd suffered a heart attack and didn't even contact the police, but word soon leaked of the suicide.

News reports blamed Chester's worries about Pittsburgh, and that's what Dean Bricker heard: "He let that play on his mind. He had heard so often as advice that he couldn't compete with Reick's . . . and he thought they were going to go bankrupt."

Chester's daughters Margaret and Helen said there were numerous factors. Helen explained, "It was a big step, and I'm not sure that he was quite comfortable with his [youngest] brother being the head of it yet. This was such a big undertaking for a 25-year-old." Also, Chester's sister Josephine Bricker spent much of her life at the state asylum in Massillon, which is why, Helen said, "My father would say to my mother, 'Don't let them put me in Massillon,' and I think this is what he was afraid of. They're an unusual family in many ways. Stress was very difficult for all of them."

Growing up away from their roots in Mansfield, neither daughter felt close to the rest of the Isalys, "and for us," said Helen, "it was even less than that after our father died." Compounding the situation, Helen recalled, was that her mother said they hadn't received all the Pittsburgh stock that was due Chester: "A breach came with us and the rest of them, although my mother would never speak ill of anybody. . . . They say she was the largest Isaly family stockholder, and she got some of Pittsburgh, but not what was set aside for her." Margaret added, "I don't know whether she blamed lawyers or what; there were some lawyers involved in this too. She believed they were bought off. But who knows?"

Samuel took over as Youngstown manager, and Charles replaced Samuel as president. Plans proceeded in Pittsburgh, and the Boulevard was complete by spring 1931. It was about then that Samuel had a visit from Claire "Larry" Hatch, a bold 25-year-old who, perhaps more than anyone, determined the course of Isaly's for the next quarter century. He gained fame later for starting another regionally famous company, but he was very private and shunned publicity. Hatch never granted interviews—except once, to talk to this author about Isaly's.

Hatch was a regular at an Isaly's while working as a manager for Scott stores near Youngstown: "Isaly's only supplied the dairy products to the franchises, and as a result, the managers of the stores were interrupted constantly by salesmen coming in for coffee and candy and canned goods and what not. So I talked to the manager of the Struthers store and I asked him if he thought there was any room for a cooperative of buying for 15 or 20 of the stores, everything except dairy products. And he said yes, he'd be glad to get rid of all these salesmen that were pestering him. So I went and talked to 12 of the Isaly's franchise people, and the fellow in Farrell, Pennsylvania, asked me if I'd checked this out with Isaly's. I said, 'No, they only sell you dairy products and they couldn't care less.' 'Well,' he said, 'they're kind of funny people. If I were you I'd go and talk to them.'

"So I talked to Sam Isaly . . . and he said, 'If you can do this for these franchises, how would you like to come to work for us?' So we worked out a deal, and I went to work in Youngstown. In the morning I would stick around the office and see what was going on, and in the afternoon Sam would take me out to these stores. There were stores that had peanut roasters with stovepipes out the front window, so the smell would come out on the sidewalk. They were a mess, they really were.

Don't Get Married!

If Isaly's had its way, Joan Lutz might not be here. Her parents, Herman and Lucille Lutz, met while working at the Homestead, Pennsylvania, Isaly's in the early 1930s. "When Mother brought Dad—Hermie—home to her family of five younger brothers and sisters, they were so impressed with Dad, for he made the meatloaf at Isaly's with the hard-boiled egg inside, which they thought was just about as clever as you could get." But there was a problem: "My parents were secretly married in West Virginia, for Isaly's did not permit employees to date." It being the depression, they continued living with their families to keep their secret (and their jobs). "It took a year, but their marriage was discovered, and they were fired."

"So after about two weeks of this, he told me they were opening a new plant in Pittsburgh, and how would I like to go down there for a week or 10 days and get an idea on what the latest word in dairy plants was. . . . What he came down to do was to find out if Henry Isaly would take me on as manager of stores here, because Sam was afraid I would upset his franchise dealers so that there'd be hell to pay."

They didn't speak of those times until 15 years later: "Henry and I used to go out on Saturday nights and see what was going on in the stores and how they were taking care of things. We had two stores in East Liberty; one was in a building I owned. . . . I parked on Penn Avenue, and before we got out of the car, Henry put his hand on my knee and said, 'Did you ever know how close you were to getting fired?' and I said 'no.' He said, 'Sam told me when you came to Pittsburgh, "That guy Hatch is too much of a fireball. He'll ruin the franchises."'"

Indeed, Hatch gained a reputation for being blunt, such as when describing Henry Isaly: "He was a wonderful man, but he just had that one terrible shortcoming. He just couldn't see the future. . . . The Isalys had a marvelous knack of making wonderful dairy products, but they didn't know business at all. I can remember the Braddock restaurant. . . . The payroll was 28 percent, and the gross profit was 18 percent."

So Hatch came to Pittsburgh and was put in charge of its six stores: "It took me almost three years to get the stores back in the black after they'd been run by a bunch of farmers. The thing was just a mess. They had an older fellow out in Homestead . . . he'd make the girls come up to his office so he could look up their rear ends and so on before he'd pay them off."

Hatch said he brought the store managers together when he started: "I called them all in one afternoon and marched them into Henry Isaly's office, and in essence I told them, if I told them to sell piss pots at the curb, they were going to sell piss pots at the curb and that was it, and I turned them loose. But there wasn't a one of them that lasted."

A New Store Every Week

PAUL CLEVER WORKED IN THE YOUNGSTOWN ICE CREAM DEPARTMENT WHILE attending college. Just before Chester Isaly died, he told Clever that Pittsburgh would need an ice cream maker, so Clever quit school: "It was during the depression. It was getting really tough, so I thought I might as well take a job where I could. . . . I got there several months ahead, and I'd look out on this big parking lot—there wouldn't be anybody there, you know—and you'd just wonder whether there would ever come a time when they'd be crowded." Clever would later marry one of the dozen "Klondike girls" making the plant's 10,000 daily bars.

The Boulevard salesroom opened May 18, 1931. In one evening, its 30 scoopers made 12,000 cones: That's one every two seconds for a solid six hours. "When Isaly's hit Pittsburgh," says Krohe, "they just turned the town upside down, 'cause this was something new. . . . You got four ounces of good ice cream for 5¢—you couldn't turn it down. And people didn't turn it down; they flocked in those stores." Hatch agreed: "There were a few mom and pop stores, but there weren't dairy stores that had everything from cottage cheese to buttermilk to ice cream."

Clever listed another draw: "Mr. Isaly believed in giving the customer a little bit more, and sometimes in the wintertime we'd put more cream in their milk and we'd have a bigger top on our bottle of milk. People appreciated that. Our ice cream was, almost all year-round, 12 percent butterfat," versus the typical 10 percent. As Henry Isaly once said, "Why not give the public a break, particularly so if they are willing to come to your place of business to buy your products—and pay you cash for them?"

Just what made Isaly's so special? How about 48 cans of ice cream? H. WILLIAM ISALY

His brother Samuel Isaly used Pittsburgh's opening to reinvent Isaly's stores. He surveyed the three Ohio branches with company architect Clyde "Shooey" Schuemacher (not to be confused with later company

Though homey, Isaly's Ohio stores were less standardized than their Pennsylvania counterparts. Note the cone display above the telephone and the circa 1940 Wurlitzer tabletop jukebox on the right. MAHONING VALLEY HISTORICAL SOCIETY, YOUNGSTOWN, OHIO

architect Vincent Schoeneman). What they found, Shooey wrote, "was pretty sad—dark half cases, dark wall refrigerators with the glass doors painted so that people could not see inside, dark oiled floors, no ventilators." Samuel directed him to design a store to address these problems: a "natural merchandiser, where the poor as well as the well-to-do would shop and feel at home. Above all, it must be the smartest store on the street and different from anything else."

Shooey locked himself away for six weeks: "There were no full-length cases made, so we designed one, firmly believing if merchandise was worth storing, it was worth displaying." Facades were also studied: "Fronts of marble and bronze which cost thousands did not stand out above brick and other fronts." White glass was chosen—nonporous, so it was easy to clean, and new, so it was eye-catching. Originally used was West Virginia–made Vitrolite, but after problems with fading, Isaly's switched to Carrara glass made by Pittsburgh Plate Glass (PPG).

Pittsburgh's inaugural store in Homewood served as a "laboratory" for two months. Refinements that emerged included stainless steel countertops, rounded white buttermilk tanks, and aluminum chairs made by Pittsburgh-based Alcoa. Air conditioning was tried and soon spread chainwide.

The company spent $1.5 million over five years: Even franchises were redone at no charge. While the depression was closing other businesses, Isaly's reported that every store's sales gained 20 to 42 percent.

Ice Cream Outlets

When Isaly's opened its Pittsburgh plant, ice cream was rarely sold at dairy or deli stores like the ones the company was opening. Here's a partial breakdown of ice cream sales by outlet for 1932:

Drugstores	36.0%
Confectioneries	19.4%
Groceries	11.5%
Bakeries	10.2%
Restaurants	9.4%
Ice cream parlors	9.3%
Delicatessens	2.4%

Source: A. J. Claxton, "Retail Outlets," *Abstracts of Literature on the Manufacture and Distribution of Ice Cream* (Harrisburg, PA: Intl. Assn. of Ice Cream Mfrs., 1933).

U.S. ice cream consumption sagged through the 1930s—after peaking at 465 million gallons in 1929, it tumbled to 148 million by 1933. Still, Isaly's prospered. The Youngstown plant payroll jumped in those years from 66 to 180, and a $100,000 addition was under way. Satellite plants opened to serve Akron in 1934 and Canton in 1935.

Pittsburgh had to enlarge the Boulevard three years after opening, and by 1937, it was supplying 60 Isaly's. Dorothy Keim, who feared that the floor

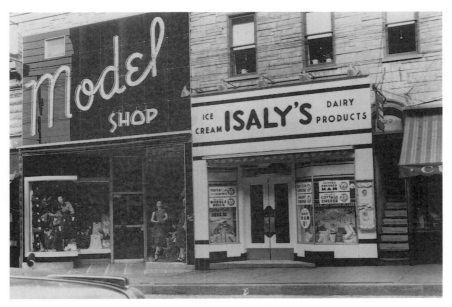

Pittsburgh-branch stores aimed for a modern, uniform look. Here, the Canonsburg Isaly's storefront shows off trendy art deco lettering. MRS. RALPH M. McAFEE

Children especially loved when Isaly's opened a new plant. This was East Market Street in Akron, June 20, 1934. MAHONING VALLEY HISTORICAL SOCIETY, YOUNGSTOWN, OHIO

The opening of the Canton plant saw 40,000 descend on West Tuscarawas Street, and 600 gallons of ice cream were given away. From left, John Mahon (Selma Isaly's husband), William R., Samuel, Charles, Marian, Nick White from the Mansfield plant, Henry, and architect Clyde "Shooey" Schuemacher. WILLIAM R. ISALY

would give way when the Evans Avenue Isaly's opened in McKeesport, Pennsylvania, explained the attraction: "In 1935, there wasn't much excitement in our lives. You didn't have television. There were some movies, but not everybody could afford to go. Life was kind of dull because there wasn't much money to enjoy the better things, and to have a store open was a big deal."

Krohe said it was the mill towns that made the company a success: "Henry made leases in rundown towns like Braddock, Duquesne, and McKeesport in the depression. You had your pick of six or eight places. They were rundown, and Isaly's would remodel with new roofs, kitchens. . . . A lot were old theaters with slanty floors." Isaly's could rent for as little as $50 a month, but Larry Hatch thought Henry Isaly was missing the obvious: "He was a farmer, and he couldn't make anything too good. . . . He was in Millvale, Turtle Creek, towns that just had no future. . . . We had 35 restaurants before he agreed to go downtown and pay $350 a month rent on Liberty Avenue."

Henry's son H. William Isaly agreed, up to a point: "My dad was too conservative, he was, but you need that solid base in a company or you end up making decisions eventually that break you." When Isaly's did open in downtown Pittsburgh, it was highly successful; the Smithfield Street store, for example, was remodeled in 1946 to seat 250, with a central oval-shaped cafeteria and milk shake bar.

Hatch's firm supervision helped keep the high standards set by the Isalys. In a 1937 memo, Hatch declared, "Department heads who specifically instruct clerks to skim the cream off of the special milk, add extra rich milk to coffee cream, use special blend coffee in place of Boulevard blend . . . instruct cooks to cheapen foods, excessively water soups . . . [or] 'roll' out the ice cream are deliberately cheating that customer, and violating one of our policies. *The penalty is instant dismissal.* . . . To get high sales, customers must be offered good values." This philosophy probably engendered more goodwill than the Skyscrapers and Klondikes of so many recollections.

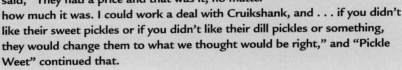

Pickle Weet

The big jars of pickles that sat atop every Isaly's counter were supplied by Lee Weet, a former salesman for Cruikshank Brothers. Weet also packaged salad dressing, olives, relish, mustard, and sweet midget pickles, all with the Weet name on them.

Why not use Pittsburgh-based Heinz? Larry Hatch said, "They had a price and that was it, no matter how much it was. I could work a deal with Cruikshank, and . . . if you didn't like their sweet pickles or if you didn't like their dill pickles or something, they would change them to what we thought would be right," and "Pickle Weet" continued that.

Isaly's as Social Center

When an Isaly's opened in Salem, Ohio, in 1932, it became the heart of the town's social life. "People entered this place of business with smiles on their faces," said town historian Dale Shaffer, "and left the same way. It wasn't just their white hats and friendliness. When the store was swarming with people after a football game, you would often see off-duty clerks pitch in to help serve customers. They probably did this for no pay, but simply out of a warm feeling for the store."

George Krohe said Hatch took special pride in a certain thin-sliced meat: "Mr. Hatch always had a running battle between the cow and the pig. Henry was the cow with dairy products, and he was the pig with the chipped ham."

Hatch explained that it started with spiced ham: "There was a Hormel general sales manager by the name of Sam McDowell, and he kept bringing six-pound cans . . . we'd slice it and it was just too tough. . . . He came out one time with a piece and I tried it out in the back and it was still too tough . . . and that weekend we were running dried beef . . . and it was being chipped on a regular slicer and the lightbulb came on in my head and I said let's try this chipped. And it was a different product completely. It was tender and sweet and so on. And within three years we were taking in more money from chipped ham sales than we were from ice cream sales. We bought an electric chipper for every restaurant, some of them had two. . . . When I left Isaly's, we were getting two 52,000-pound carloads of chipped ham a week.

"With chipped ham, you can make it as cheap as you want by adding more fat. Now we bought ham that was 8 percent fat always,

Chipped ham was easier to make after Isaly's began equipping stores with U.S. Berkel model 910 slicers, and its appeal grew with returning World War II GIs who were used to Spam. Eventually, processors changed the name of spiced ham to chopped ham; stores since have advertised "chipped chopped ham." In a 1979 article, H. William Isaly recommended using the leanest ham and setting the slicer to "0," the finest setting, then picking it up with tongs and placing it gently on wax paper: "It's like making a martini. Do it gently, so you don't bruise it." WILLIAM R. ISALY

but Donahoe's was buying 15 percent fat and chipping it in its window on Fourth Avenue. Every percentage point of fat that went into it, you could reduce the price of the chipped ham 1¢ or 2¢ a pound wholesale. It was cheaper ham, and it was always greasy." Isaly's ads from 1938 show chipped ham for 39¢ a pound.

Isaly's executive Jack Donohue remembered chipped ham's origins somewhat differently in a 1983 article: "In 1932, the Decker Meat Company, a Midwest meat-packing firm which did business with Isaly's, got the idea of concocting a ham product to make use of muscle and fat trimmings left over when hogs' legs were shaped into hams." But Donahoe couldn't, or wouldn't, say who'd had the insight to slice it thin. Henry's son H. William once said that it was proposed by a salesman for Wilson Packing Company. Krohe summed up: "It wasn't Mr. Hatch's idea at all. He was part of it, but you see so many things like that happen with Isaly's. So many people gave us ideas, and a lot of times we took credit for having thought it up ourselves, and we didn't think of everything."

In its early days, the Skyscraper was simply the Isaly cone. JUNE V. ISALY

Another product surrounded by myth is Isaly's tall cone, which would gain fame as the Skyscraper. It looked like its name—a streamlined art deco high-rise—towering four inches above the cone. Though William Isaly was selling tall cones in the teens, the scoop to make them wasn't patented until 1935 by Samuel Jennings Jr., a manufacturer located about 10 miles from Isaly's Youngstown plant in Masury, Ohio.

Jennings's daughter Pamela Grell said, "Many people were asking to buy the spoon, and Sam Isaly became very upset because he had the corner on the market, so to speak. To calm him down, my dad delivered the patent to him." The patent is assigned to the Isaly Dairy Company of Youngstown, though it never mentions "Skyscraper" or that it's a scoop or a dipper; rather, the patent calls it a spoon.

Jennings designed and manufactured much more for Isaly's, including packing spoons, soda fountain coils, and 800-gallon milk tanks. Pamela's sister even saw Sam Isaly and her dad tinker with an automated Klondike machine. Jennings also improved the 40- and 48-hole ice cream cabinets called Ackermans, named for original builder Mike Ackerman of Mansfield, Ohio. They were revolutionary for holding so many cans and keeping ice cream the same consistency throughout each can.

Art Frank, hired in 1935 by William Isaly's nephew Eugene Isaly, heard that the scoop developed by accident: "They weren't going fast enough with the dippers and they were breaking, so somebody just grabbed a big serving spoon like they have in restaurants. That thing worked all right, so they pounded it a little bit this way and that, and it evolved." But some Skyscraper scoops are embossed "Rainbow" where "Isaly" is usually found. Don Flowers, who worked for Rieck-McJunkin and Keystone Cone, said the Rainbow Dipping Spoon Company made these, and a 1929 ad in *Ice Cream Trade Journal* confirms it. Still, Isaly's had been making tall cones since the teens.

Krohe explained the technique to scooping a Skyscraper: "There was a place for every cone to come out of a can in a properly run Isaly's store. You'd start a new can by looking at it to your left. Counterclockwise you'd have to cut six cones out. That would take you almost halfway around the can. Then you'd come out and pick up all the ones that were left in that half circle. Then you made all the rest of the cones crossways." A chart below the counter showing 18 circles in a can helped new hires. A manager would know if the clerks were scooping correctly by checking the can for the pattern.

Glenn Fehr started at Isaly's in 1935 when he was 15: "They taught you to make Skyscrapers by taking you to the basement, where there was an ice cream cabinet, and they'd give you a full can of vanilla ice cream and an empty can and you'd have to scoop the ice cream and put it on a cone and weigh it. It was difficult; you'd get too little or too much. You'd keep practicing until you'd developed the wrist movement."

Pamela Grell believes that this is the first day of the Skyscraper scoop, designed by her father, Sam Jennings. Store supervisor Carl Rafoth is scooping the cones at the Youngstown plant salesroom while Grell's dad watches (at Rafoth's immediate right). PAMELA GRELL

The Scoop on Scoops

Until 1878, no one saw a need for ice cream scoops—big spoons worked just fine—but once a scoop was introduced, an avalanche followed. The first scoop, or dipper, took two hands: one to hold the scoop, and the other to turn a key to remove the ice cream. The one-handed dipper came in the 1890s, and most models afterward had a thumb action to remove the ice cream. When novelties like Eskimo Pie and Klondike debuted around 1920, dippers were produced to cut ice cream into blocks or other shapes. Then in 1935, the Zeroll dipper revolutionized the industry with its practical and sanitary one-piece design. Yes, Skyscrapers had been made for years with a one-piece scoop, but they required the hard-to-master "cutting" technique.

Source: Wayne Smith, *Ice Cream Dippers* (Walkersville, MD: Wayne Smith, 1986).

The Reverend Robert Bricker scooped during high school in his dad's Isaly's in Youngstown: "If you got them too big you lost money and cracked the cone. If you made them too small they slid down in the cone and people didn't think they were getting their money's worth. . . . I sweated more drops of sweat into the ice cream cans in that store than I ever hoped to."

Russell Stevenson, who worked at the Boulevard, said, "Not a few new hires were let go when after some days they couldn't cut a proper Isaly cone. I could cut and hold 10 cones in one hand. . . . One or two could even manage 12 cones!"

Bard's Dairy Stores in Pittsburgh responded by marketing a tall cone and a Klondike clone and even copied Isaly's facades. Rodgers Dairy, an offshoot of Brass Rail restaurants, also copied Isaly's facade but added a picture of its Skyscraper imitator. Both were often located near Isaly's, sometimes even next door.

Isaly's surveyed its stores again in 1936. This time, architect Shooey reported, "There are copies. The owners admit they are copies. That seems to be the penalty we are having to pay for leadership—but we lead."

• • •

One writer described Walter Paulo, a nephew of William Isaly, as "never satisfied with a job that is being done well. He always thinks it can be done better." Among his innovations were Whitehouse ice cream (vanilla with cherries, developed in 1919 for Washington's Birthday to boost sales in February) and Chocolate Bubble ice cream (nuts, chocolate syrup, and whipped cream wrapped in ice cream).

Paulo was just 13 when he began delivering milk for Isaly's in 1915. At age 19, he and his brother crossed America selling "Paulo's Magic Cleaner," guaranteed to clean anything as well as soap and water—because that's what it was. He returned to Mansfield no richer, but by 1931, he had worked up to Youngstown plant *and* stores manager.

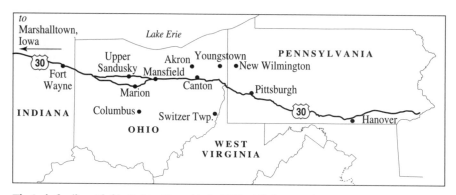

The Isaly family settled in Switzer Township in 1833. A little more than a century later, Isaly's was operating eleven plants. With the opening of Hanover Klondike in 1978, the last of the eleven dairies closed.

Butter was a huge seller, so in 1934, the Youngstown division secured a steady supply by purchasing Chief Dairy in Upper Sandusky, Ohio, which produced 1.5 million pounds of butter annually. Paulo was put in charge of its expansion, and Chief was soon producing 2 million pounds of butter plus American cheese, cheddar cheese, and condensed milk. Like at Isaly's other plants, generations worked side by side: Jean Moon's dad worked at Chief from 1919 until passing away on the job in 1968, her three brothers worked there, and she and her mom made the plant's cheesecloths at home. In 1938, the Youngstown division also purchased the New Wilmington Cheese Company.

Pittsburgh originally made its own butter, but Paul Clever said, "Those big churns are enormous, so it was easier for us to buy our butter." In 1936, Pittsburgh acquired Schlosser's Creamery Products of Fort Wayne, Indiana, known for its Oak Grove butter and "Chillie bars," a Klondike cousin. Schlosser's became Isaly's Creamery Products in 1938.

Ruth Stinnett worked the butter room at Isaly's Creamery in 1943: "There were six or eight girls sitting by this conveyor, and we had to grab the butter off and wrap it. On hot days this butter was pretty messy. And get this—*no* gloves!"

Is "Sweet Creamery" Butter Better?

Though it sounds more appealing, sweet creamery butter is more an explanation of the manufacturing process than of the product. The length of time that cream stands before churning makes a big difference in its taste. People used to like a strong lactic flavor, but most butter is now made from "sweet," or newly risen and pasteurized, cream.

"Creamery" refers to the dairy plant where butter is manufactured, as opposed to farm-made butter, but the elegant sound of the word is probably worth more to consumers than its literal meaning. It also implies that the milk came from a mix of hundreds of cows raised on standard feed.

Source: Margaret Visser, *Much Depends on Dinner* (New York: Grove Press, 1987).

PLANTS — STORES

ISALY'S INC.

Announces

The Opening of a New Plant

and Sales Concourse

2800 N. High Street, Columbus, Ohio

Thursday, November 19, 1936

You and your friends are cordially invited, as honorary guests, to visit and inspect this new Isaly Plant and enjoy with us the festivities attendant upon this happy opening day.

Exacting inspections, finest refrigeration and the rapid transportation of all dairy foods to our stores, insure the safety and guarantee the quality of Isaly's Milk and Dairy Products.

Pictured on the upper left of this ad is Isaly's certified dairy farm near Youngstown. WILLIAM R. ISALY

With plants covering northern Ohio, Isaly's turned south to Columbus in 1936. The new branch was to be headed by Robert Isaly, a nephew of founder William, but he died at age 33 before it was even incorporated. (His father, Henry R. Isaly, became vice-president and served on the other boards but concentrated on his own cheese business.) When the Columbus Isaly's Inc. opened, Charles Isaly was president, and son Richard was manager.

The largest remodeling started in 1938 when a $400,000 expansion at Youngstown transformed the plant into an art deco beauty of cream, tan, and green terra cotta. *Dairy World* called it "the most modern and beautiful of its kind in the country, if not in the world." Its glass block tower, lit from behind with fluorescent tubes, became a beacon for the company and the region.

Samuel, manager of the branch, explained, "We expand only when we can adequately enlarge our close supervision system and when we see a need for our service and products. We do not put ourselves in a position where we are so expanded that we cannot know exactly what is going on in all our stores all the time." Samuel was known to eat at the stores anonymously, informing them later that he'd visited.

A writer described Samuel as having "the caution of his Swiss ancestors. . . . Never have I come in contact with a man who was more cautious, painstaking, and matter of fact. . . . Isaly is about as self-sufficient and self-contained as anyone you would find in many a moon."

Samuel and Shooey designed the plant's interior, while local architect Charles Owlsley did the general structure. Owlsley had admired a mural by Carlo Ciampaglia at the New York World's Fair and commissioned him to paint a dairy-themed series for the new lobby. The building was paneled with

The renovated Youngstown plant shows off its streamlined deco facade. SAMUEL D. ISALY

woods from around the globe, among them Mexican primavera, African mako-ri, and Philippine paldeo. The penthouse reflected Samuel's love of deep-sea fishing, with life preservers, pilots' wheels, deck chairs, and a linoleum floor inlaid with a mariner's compass.

／ Many remember listening to radio broadcasts of Susie Side-Saddle and Marjorie Mariner originating from the fifth-floor auditorium. School groups also had lunch there after touring Isaly's and Ward's Bakery across the street. Klondikes on a stick were churned out at 3,000 per hour, while 85 trucks handled home and store deliveries.

As part of the publicity campaign, a map was issued in 1939 picturing the company's "Milky Way" of 310 stores. A second version included a count: Akron, 27; Canton, 14; Columbus, 24; Mansfield, 21; Marion, 21; Pittsburgh, 74; and Youngstown, 129.

The Pittsburgh branch also sponsored a show that year that most just called "Radio Basket Night." It featured the George Hyde orchestra and four women called the Swiss Maids, a nod to Isaly's Swiss heritage. The music, however, was overshadowed by the giving away of "bulging baskets of food" at a random store. Larry Hatch recalled, "Near the end of the program, we had Hyde call out the name of the restaurant, and the trucks would leave the dairy with [up to] 600 baskets." People began shadowing the basket truck, and the show was canceled after one season for fear of harm coming to the stores and customers.

Though Isaly's was prospering, the economy was still tight. William Francis started at a New Castle, Pennsylvania, Isaly's for 25¢ an hour but says, "There were probably 200 people that would take my job if I didn't want it." Bill Pfleghar was hired at New Brighton, Pennsylvania: "Jobs were very scarce in 1937, but I had pull, so I lucked out. We were paid 25¢ an hour, and you had to work the first two weeks for nothing." Julia (Bozick) Clark says that when she began working at the East Palestine, Ohio, Isaly's in 1940, it "paid 18¢ an hour. My first pay for two weeks was $18.67 and I was very happy to have a job."

Ruth Semones was a teenager: "My dad died in a coal mine at Windsor Heights, West Virginia. Mom had a breakdown. We three kids had a rough time. Mom got $15 and us three kids got $5 each a month. . . . I went to Isaly's, got my first job. I was so proud to work there. We had clean uniforms. We wore hair nets, we had to, and we had to get a health card. Back then I think I got $27 a week. . . . Isaly's did wonders for me."

Les Wagner, who walked 18 miles round-trip to earn 30¢ an hour in Ambridge, Pennsylvania, remembered, "There was a couple about 40 years old that came in regularly. Their order was always the same: one dill pickle for 4¢. They

The Louisville, Ohio, Isaly's opened about 1940. WILLIAM R. ISALY

would ask me to cut it in half, give them two pieces of wax paper and two glasses of water. They would sit in a booth, pick up the pickle halves in the wax paper, eat their 'snack,' drink their water, and leave."

In 1942, a heart attack claimed Charles, the second of the four Isaly brothers to die young. Henry became president of Pittsburgh, as did Samuel in Youngstown (turning over his general manager position to Walter Paulo). Charles's son Richard, already managing Columbus, took over as manager and treasurer at Marion. Less than two months later, Columbus reduced its dividend rate and the value of common stock shares from $25 to $5, the first signs of slippage in 40 years. A year later, company cofounder Jesse Isaly died, leaving his son Ruhland as Mansfield treasurer and general manager, with his other son Robert assisting.

Now deep into World War II, Isaly's pitched in by sending products overseas: 2.4 million pounds of dry milk, 2.7 million pounds of butter, and 4.3 million pounds of cheese. Ralph McAfee recalled that butter became so precious that his Canonsburg, Pennsylvania, Isaly's got only 60 pounds a week: "We'd open the store at six o'clock, and I always had a line two blocks long for people who wanted a half pound of butter. The police would have two officers stationed out front to let in the customers. . . . It was gone the first 25, 30 minutes."

Jack McGeary said that the small amounts of butter his store received were reserved for regular customers: "You would put the butter in the coffee bag or

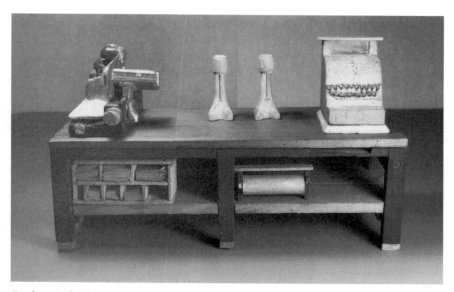

Employee Jack McGeary carved a store interior from Isaly's discarded cheese boxes. In addition to a deli case, steam table, and workers, he made this counter, which shows a manual slicer adapted to chip ham. "After they came out with the chipper," said Jack, "I used to go to bed and say my prayers and say thank God for the man that invented the chipper, 'cause boy that saved me a lot of work." PHOTO BY THE AUTHOR

any kind of container and sell it that way, but you wouldn't dare let anybody know that you had butter in the store." In Donora, Pennsylvania, a truck unloader took his entire pay in butter.

Butter remained precious after the war, too, because returning servicemen, their eating habits changed, consumed more milk, ice cream, and cottage cheese. In 1945, Isaly's Youngstown branch purchased the Marshall Creamery in Marshalltown, Iowa, for its butter and cheese. Though it was 700 miles west, transport was eased by its being on the transcontinental Lincoln Highway (U.S. Route 30), like most of the Isaly's plants.

Isaly's Victory Brick celebrated the end of World War II with a red raspberry V running the length of the ice cream. But the company found a new competitor after the war: convenience stores. When Lawson's began opening in Akron, Isaly's responded by cutting milk prices from 18¢ a quart to 16¢, but it still couldn't match Lawson's 14¢, probably because fewer workers were needed at the new-type stores. Still Isaly's continued growing, and by 1947, each division had gained stores compared with the count made eight years earlier: Akron had added 8; Canton, 11; Columbus, 26; Mansfield, 5; Marion, 4; Pittsburgh, 21; and Youngstown, 11.

More expansion was planned, but in fact, the chain's 400 stores was its peak. Though stores continued opening, just as many were closing at the territory's fringes. "Isaly's best year was 1947," recalled Larry Hatch. "From that time on, it slowly went down."

Milk and Its Uses

Ice cream is just one of the many uses for milk. In Isaly's heyday, ice cream used up only one-twentieth of milk production. Here's a national breakdown for 1948:

Creamery butter	21.1%
Farm butter	5.0%
Cheese	9.2%
Condensed and evaporated milk	6.9%
Ice cream	5.1%
Dry milk, cream, and malted milk	1.6%
Household use	48.0%
Fed to calves	2.6%
Waste and miscellany	0.5%

Source: J. H. Frandsen and D. Horace Nelson, *Ice Creams and Other Frozen Deserts* (Amherst, MA: J. H. Frandsen, 1950).

Part of the decline can be traced to the early death of yet another brother, Samuel, from heart disease late in 1946. Samuel's legacy, as an editorial said, was "an industry which distributed necessities so efficiently as to raise the standard of living in the communities it serves." The company, so dependent on the personalities of William Isaly's four sons, was losing its core strength.

A new Marion plant opened in August 1947, two stories of reinforced concrete and glass brick with a "cold core" of refrigerated rooms. The publicity barrage led to Isaly's giving away 24,000 Skyscrapers on opening day. The plant served 23 company stores and some 90 dealers who retailed Isaly products. Although it featured the latest in automated milk and butter production, Klondikes were still made by hand: Pans were filled, the frozen slabs cut into bars, and the bars hooked and dipped. WILLIAM R. ISALY

Henry Isaly and "Alice in Dairyland" eye a tableful of cheese. GAYLORD LAMOND

Henry Isaly became president of Pittsburgh, Youngstown, and Mansfield, but luckily for the chain, he was the perfect man for the job. His son H. William recalled, "He was a very nice looking guy with a very pleasant face and a very pleasant manner, but he was very straightforward. I mean you just knew right where you stood immediately. When people would come to negotiate their lease for the next couple of years and they owned the storeroom, they'd walk away and be so happy with their deal, and it wasn't because my dad was giving away the chef, it was just because it was such a nice experience to come and negotiate with my dad."

Paul Clever remembered, "Henry was a real nice guy, just unbelievable how nice a person he was. He hobnobbed with the Scaifes and Mellons here in Pittsburgh, and when he's around you he's just like your dad. . . . Oftentimes at lunch he'd just go down, he wouldn't bother to go out to some fancy restaurant, he'd just come down to the store and have a ham sandwich and a milk shake."

Unions were making headway at Isaly's by then. The Retail Clerks Council (AFL) signed a contract in 1946 for Youngstown's 42 company-owned stores, starting new clerks at 55¢ an hour. Peter Argentine said that Henry Isaly "made employees take active part in the union, encouraged us to attend to make sure we knew what they were doing. . . . As a union man and a man who believes in unions, I can't say enough about Henry Isaly and the Isaly family." Argentine said that when he was sick in 1944, Henry "asked if I needed money and sent a blank check."

Mary (Shubert) Dybowski said, "He gave so much to his employees. . . . He didn't care if you were black or white . . . always had a nice word, he never insulted a person. Never hollered, 'Hey, get out there to work, what are you doing here?'" For 22 years, Dybowski did all the cooking in the Boulevard's employee cafeteria without air conditioning and only a short-order cook for help, yet she said, "It was hard work but it was enjoyable, honest it was so enjoyable. I get emotional. . . . It was so beautiful working for Isaly's."

Dybowski was on the union negotiating committee but found that she often disagreed with the demands of her union president, who wanted raises of 30¢ while Isaly's typically gave 6¢ to 10¢: "I wanted more money too, [but] I didn't want it hard on the company because he [Henry Isaly] was so good to us."

Frank Dandrea, though, felt the union had numerous problems with management. He started in 1931, working as much as 18 hours a day with no overtime, and getting token raises until the Teamsters began negotiating wages in 1937. "They worked the death out of you," recalled Dandrea. But even he admitted that few complained: "Every morning, 20 to 25 men were at shipping trying to get a job. . . . And Mr. Isaly was a real good person."

Larry Hatch saw labor from the opposite side: "We used to load the truck . . . about 6:30 or 7:00 in the morning, and it would get back from Wheeling at about 7:00 at night because they were paid by the hour. When the plant became unionized, they were paid on a commission basis, on the amount of goods that were sold. The truck came back by 1:30 or 2:00."

Shopping plazas were beginning to dot suburban roadsides by 1950, with their lure of free and easy parking, and the company followed. George Krohe said that developers sought grocery stores, banks, and "*always* an Isaly's. They wanted us because in those days your lease was their deposit on paying for these malls. . . . An Isaly lease was money in the bank because they knew they were gonna get this money."

Henry Isaly

Gil Maffeo started at the Boulevard plant in 1943 and stayed until it closed in 1978. On Gil's second day, Henry Isaly introduced himself, saying, "Welcome to my family." Later, during a drivers' strike, "People pummeled us with eggs and bricks from passing cars, and called us baby killers for not delivering milk. Henry Isaly was very worried about the plant's big glass windows, not from us, from what the people passing might do. He said, 'We may be on different sides, but this thing will be settled someday. Keep an eye on my building, it's still your home and always will be.'

"You'd think he would have been afraid to come outside to talk to us, but he came to the picket line and invited us inside the plant. He said, 'There's so much stuff back there, it will only spoil, go ahead and take anything perishable, milk or whatever.' Sure he had money, but he was an ordinary guy."

Isaly's gradually heeded the call of suburbia. Here is the 1951 grand opening of the Lane Avenue Shopping Center Isaly's in the Upper Arlington section of Columbus. H. RON CAMPBELL

Charles's son Richard, managing both Marion and Columbus, left the business in the late 1940s. Younger brother William R. had worked his way up through the branches to become president, manager, and treasurer of Columbus. Youngest brother David became manager and treasurer at Marion. Angelo Doria, the only manager the Marion salesroom ever had, has only high praise for David. But both branches were struggling.

"The Marion plant was a mess," recalled Hatch. "I went down there, and it almost made me sick. Their [store] kitchens were just a disgrace." Henry Isaly wanted George Krohe to take over managing Marion's stores, but Hatch wanted to demote Krohe, not promote him. When Henry persisted, "I said, 'good luck, take him.' So they went down and ran that into the ground, and eventually all the Isaly plants just went too."

June Isaly, a daughter-in-law of Henry's, said that Krohe "was just extremely loyal, a hard worker, classy gentleman, very principled and dedicated . . . perhaps as close to the very same kind of gentleman as Henry Isaly was." But Krohe admitted, "I could get into trouble because I had a mind of my own."

Hatch recalled that during an industrywide strike, "I made a deal to get ice cream from Wheeling. . . . Well, I found out Krohe was letting a drugstore in Bellevue where he lived, he was giving him some of the ice cream too. The only people who had ice cream was Isaly's and one drugstore in Bellevue." Krohe had bent the rules—just as Hatch did crossing state lines for ice cream.

Then the Isaly family experienced more early deaths. Mansfield general manager Ruhland Isaly committed suicide in 1952, and Charles's son David Isaly died of heart problems in 1953 at just 35 years old. George Krohe, who'd been Marion stores' supervisor for two years (despite Hatch's objections), assumed David's duties as Marion manager and treasurer.

In 1953, the Columbus Board of Health approved half-gallon milk containers. Borden's (later based in Columbus) introduced disposable cardboard cartons, while Isaly's stuck with glass bottles, claiming that they weren't as wasteful. The Columbus division dissolved a year later, less than 20 years after opening. Stores in the branch had already been closing, down from 50 to 28 in seven years. William R. Isaly moved back to preside over Marion.

Looking back on Columbus, William R. simply said, "It never developed the volume necessary to operate." His sister Marian thinks that maybe it was "because they ran into Borden's," but Bob Isaly, grandson of Columbus cheese maker Henry, said Borden's wasn't to blame: "We opened too many small units. . . . Labor is expensive, and we couldn't get enough volume. We needed fewer but bigger stores."

The 14 Columbus company stores were taken over by Marion and given a $100,000 facelift, but Krohe said, "It was very hard to come back. We remodeled some, but they never recovered. They helped tear down the Marion operation." Even a dozen managers brought from Pittsburgh couldn't help: "They were used to a first-class operation. They were paid a little better, but all I got was complaints. They were really country stores."

Pittsburgh and Youngstown, though, were still prospering. In Clairton, south of Pittsburgh, Joyce (Phillis) Link remembered the steel mills "running full blast, with shops and stores up and down Miller Avenue doing a great business. . . . Friday night after football, people were lined out the door for ice cream, and even at lunch, the store was full to overflowing."

In Youngstown, Walter Paulo had became secretary and executive vice-president after Samuel's death, in addition to being store manager. Paulo was also heavily involved in civic affairs, from championing local hospitals to promoting savings bonds. Art Frank recalled his hands-on style: In 1955, when the union asked for delivery route helpers, "Walter asked, 'What's your busiest, heaviest day?' So they told him. He says, 'OK, I'll be over at four o'clock in the morning on that day. I'm taking the truck out that has the heaviest load on it and I'm going to deliver it by myself.'" Paulo, age 53, delivered 750 cases of milk weighing 45 pounds each. When he finished ahead of schedule, the union man joked that their hours might instead be *cut*. Paulo, though, still gave them some helpers.

Another Isaly who earned the respect of employees was H. William, born Henry W. Isaly Jr. in 1931 to Henry and Louise. "The summer I remember the most, I was probably a sophomore in high school and I got to work in what they called the [Boulevard's] condensed department. In the summer when there was a flush of milk, we used to take this extra milk in and condense it. . . . It was so hot. . . . Also I was sent over to Youngstown for a summer once to work in the butter department, and that was the same type of hot, hard work."

Walter Paulo makes a TV appearance on Marjorie Mariner's "Kitchen Korner."
MAHONING VALLEY HISTORICAL SOCIETY, YOUNGSTOWN, OHIO

After college and the army, H. William returned in 1956: "Now here's where the real advantage is of being the son of the boss. . . . I was put right into our Pittsburgh plant as the assistant plant manager."

• • •

The Pittsburgh branch celebrated its silver anniversary in 1956 with a dinner awarding gold watches and pins to 21 employees who had been with the company for 25 years. Some of the awardees were women and blacks, though they'd had far less chance for advancement: The only job for black men until almost 1960 was porter, and it wasn't until 1966 that the first woman was promoted to supervisor.

Some African Americans recall Isaly's being restrictive in other ways: "We could go in and get an ice cream," recalled Donald King of Pittsburgh, "but we couldn't sit down there in the Isaly's and eat the ice cream cone. We had to go outside and take it with us." Frank Bolden said, "Everything was separate in America at that time. Discrimination and segregation was the order of the day." He said Isaly's "didn't serve Negroes at all, and then later on they did. They didn't have any [stores] in the [predominantly black] Hill District, though. They were everywhere but the Hill. They didn't have it in the ghetto."

A recent history of Youngstown recalled that even after World War II, Isaly's "refused admittance to black customers, as did most eating places downtown." But a 1937 article saw Isaly's differently: "What is good enough for the select community is none too costly for the slums. . . . Whether in slum or exclusive suburb, each [Isaly's] is an expensive investment and must justify its existence by volume sales."

Pittsburgher John Weston said, "We never experienced any prejudice in Isaly's." Born in 1936, he remembers visiting the Homewood store as a child. His older brother worked evenings at the Federal Street Isaly's as a porter, and when John got a job downtown, he ate at the Isaly's on Liberty Avenue: "There were places you couldn't go as a young black man, but Isaly's was one of the places you'd feel comfortable." As a mailman, Weston became a daily customer

William Francis Remembers

William J. Francis started in New Castle, Pennsylvania, at 17 and recalls almost every detail from his 30-plus years with Isaly's. Here are just a few:

- The famous Isaly Klondike was made in six flavors over the years, four chocolate coated—vanilla, chocolate, maple, and vanilla Krispy coated. There was also a strawberry ice cream coated with strawberry and a butterscotch coated with butterscotch.
- Each store was graded each month. The best grade was a double-A, which had to do with profit; this paid the manager $20. To get a double-A, there had to be a 20-point spread between the store payroll and the store gross profit. For example: 12 percent payroll and 32 percent gross profit = 20-point spread.
- Walter H. Paulo, general manager of the Youngstown plant, visited each store once a month to deliver bonus checks, give advice, and inspect the store. The supervisor always leaked the day Paulo would arrive; then the manager [Francis] and assistant manager would bust our guts to get everything shipshape. If the inspection was good, each one was given two silver dollars. As I look back now, that was a pretty neat trick to get the stores in good shape once a month for $4.
- Sherwin Williams Paint Company made an "Isaly Green" paint because Isaly's used so much of it. I saw cans with that label. Green was the store color early on (1937–42), then new stores used a brown and tan color. We remodeled our store in 1956, and they were using blue at that time.

In 1948, Francis and his wife were offered an Isaly's in Minerva.

- The price was $5,000 for the store and equipment plus $550 for the merchandise inventory. "Isaly's paid the former owner this amount, then asked me to put $1,000 down and pay $50 a month to Isaly's, and they would not charge me any interest until I had it half paid off, at which [time] I received a bill for $13.50 interest. So I paid off the balance and paid only $13.50 interest on the deal."

at the Federal Street Isaly's, but he did recall "that even in the '50s, most blacks were employed as busboys or custodial, not sales clerks."

Weston's cousin George Aston was an Isaly's employee for 43 years: "They were very strict, very disciplined, [but] we also had fun—it was like a family." He's had an "Isaly's walk" ever since, "a crisp walk." He said, "I always considered myself the best porter Isaly's ever had. That was my pride. People [shrugged], 'What's a porter?' But if another manager ever came in the store, he'd say, 'what a clean store,' and my manager would say, 'I have the best porter in the world,' and that meant a lot."

Isaly's approached Aston once about managing: "The Homewood store was going down. Blacks in the neighborhood wanted a black manager." But when the acting manager told him about rampant stealing and threats, Aston turned it down. They told him he'd get lots of publicity being Isaly's first black manager, but he didn't want to be a token promotion in a troubled store.

"There were three positions in Isaly's: head clerk, assistant manager, and manager—I thought I could have done any of them. . . . I had the knowledge, the experience, but that's the way society was. It would bother me. Guys [would be] promoted in the company, then they asked me, 'Help me with this ice cream order' or 'How much pop do you order?' They respected me, but I just couldn't get the promotion. If I were a white boy, I'd have had that promotion years and years and years ago."

Krohe said that Henry Isaly wasn't enthusiastic about promoting blacks and that even into the 1950s, some Isaly's "had four dressing rooms, two for girls, two for men . . . no intermingling at all. That was so typical of the time . . . we were absolutely wrong." Isaly's was soon cited, and it was Krohe's job to resolve the matter with the city's human relations board: "I tried to talk it over and tried to make a deal of it and so forth, [telling the board], 'We had to have [clerks with] such and such character, we had to have class, we had to do this and that,' and I remember [councilman] Lou Mason said to me, 'Mr. Krohe, I presume you have to be Phi Beta Kappa to work for Isaly's.' He was ready to put the slammer on us . . . and I said to Lou, 'I have problems, but I'll give you my word I will do what I can to straighten this out.' He said, 'That's not good enough.'"

Krohe said the policies were a reflection of the times, not the people: "We had some of the finest black people I could have ever known work for us. We treated them right. Then they lasted for years, like 20, 30 years with us, and each year they'd get a little bit of an increase, and pretty soon, a little bit of an increase after 30 years gets pretty good, so they had good jobs. They were bright young people when they started with us, and 30 years older they were still bright people, and they knew all the ins and outs and they were real key people in our organization."

Hatch said the company never avoided black areas, but it's true that none were being hired as clerks. Then Isaly's "finally agreed to put, it seems to me, four stores with colored salespersons, but it fizzled out because actually in those days the customers would walk past a colored salesperson to go to a white salesperson."

Isaly's Versus Sealtest

David Rotthoff, who worked the Boulevard store, recalls a surprise phone call from Henry Isaly in the winter of 1960: "He told me to start hand-packing four quarts of ice cream. He said that he'd be in from the airport in about an hour, and he wanted the ice cream packed in dry ice to take back to Florida. . . . He was staying at the same hotel as was the vice-president of Sealtest, and they had made a bet as to which company made the better ice cream. Mr. Isaly flew up north to get what he needed to settle the bet. A few weeks later, when he returned, I asked who won the bet. His answer was, 'I did, of course.'"

David Rotthoff said that when he started at the Boulevard store in 1958, "the only blacks who worked for Isaly's worked in the kitchen. The store manager, Walter Weyman, was being pressured to put a black behind the counter as a sales clerk. Mr. Weyman called me aside and asked me if I thought one particular kitchen worker might be accepted by the other sales clerks, or whether having a black on the sales floor would cause problems. The person in question was a fellow Wilkinsburg High classmate, Alexander Burt Martin, who I had brought into the company in the first place. Alex, or 'Bucky,' was a super person, and virtually everyone in the store liked him a lot. I told Mr. Weyman that I didn't see any problems, and that same day I was given the job of training Bucky as a sales clerk. There were no problems; he did an excellent job, as I knew he would."

ICE CREAM
KLONDIKES

The Biggest Bargain in Town!

6 for 1.49

28¢ EACH _{PLUS TAX}

America's favorite ice cream bar . . .
rich vanilla ice cream with a thick, tasty coating
chocolate. Choose plain or krispy.

Different Solutions for a Different Era

TO RAISE CAPITAL, YOUNGSTOWN SOLD ITS DELIVERY TRUCKS AND CHIEF DAIRY in 1958, but there were positive signs, too: Six stores had recently opened in Cleveland. A new threat, however, had arisen in the form of fast-food restaurants.

Isaly's had ignored the trend since it had come knocking in 1948, when Larry Hatch had seen Frisch's highly successful Big Boy drive-ins in Cincinnati. A year later, Hatch too became a Big Boy franchisee, calling his chain Eat'n Park. The first restaurant had just 13 seats, but the big draw was the 10 carhops, the first in Pittsburgh. Hatch was reportedly so nervous on opening day that he threw up, but car-loving baby boomers overwhelmed the place, and it had to close after six hours to regroup. Harry Larabee remembered all the Isaly's supervisors working the opening: "It was a little bit embarrassing to Henry Isaly. . . . I was a soda jerk, some of them were cooking, and some of them were parking lot."

Once Hatch had a couple open, he offered Eat'n Park to Henry Isaly, "but he said, 'I don't want any part of them, you'll go broke the first winter.' . . . By 1956, I had eight, and Isaly's was going downhill all the time, slightly, not in any noticeable amount, but I could tell that they weren't going anywhere. . . . I tried to take them in the direction of getting stores in outlying areas where people could park, and Henry wouldn't go for it. The malls were just starting, and you could tell they were going to knock the devil out of towns like Turtle Creek and Millvale."

By 1960, there were 27 Eat'n Parks, and Hatch had left Isaly's. In spite of unpredictable weather and uncomfortable eating conditions, Americans embraced drive-in restaurants. Henry's son H. William said, "If my dad had said, 'Yeah, let's go with it,' we could have also had Isaly Eat'n Park–type stores, and Claire Hatch would've been involved and happy and would've stayed with the company." But former Isaly's supervisor Chuck Krause said that Henry was never convinced: "He'd rather sell

By the 1960s, most Klondikes were sold in take-home packs.
AUTHOR'S COLLECTION

Bring Your Family
to
Eat'n Park

2209 Saw Mill Run Boulevard
Opening Sunday, June 5th, 2:00 P.M.
Pittsburgh's First Modern Eat-in-your-Car Food Service

a quart of ice cream and a pound of chipped ham because they manufactured it, so a drive-in restaurant wasn't what he wanted."

Isaly's had another chance a few years later when Ray Kroc approached the dairy looking for $250,000 to invest in his fledgling drive-in chain, McDonald's. Kroc knew Isaly's from his years selling paper cups and Multimixers in the midwest. This gave him first-hand knowledge of soft-serve drive-ins usurping soda fountain business; the early 1950s saw Liquid Carbonic scrapping its soda fountain division and Walgreen's pulling soda fountains from its drug stores. Kroc reasoned that if soft serves were changing food habits, something more mainstream like hamburgers could revolutionize the industry. His franchising of McDonald's was of course a hit, but cash poor at first. Bob Isaly, of the Columbus cheese chain, said his dad, Paul, was all for investing, but when Isaly's Youngtown board voted, it was 4 to 3 against.

Most of the 16 Isaly's that opened in 1960 were in shopping centers—the new Isaly's in Pittsburgh's East Hills Plaza was even considered the largest dairy store in the world. Isaly's was said to be the biggest family-owned and -operated food chain in the country, but another death brought more changes. Henry

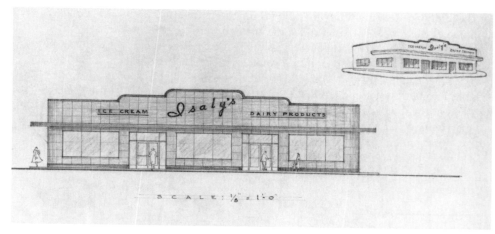

Larry Hatch bought a piece of land on Pittsburgh's Saw Mill Run Boulevard for Isaly's to take advantage of roadside commerce. Henry Isaly eventually had Hatch sell the property, so Hatch purchased it himself for a still-thriving Eat'n Park. This is one of the few renderings of the Isaly's plan that survive. ARCHITECTURE ARCHIVES, CARNEGIE MELLON UNIVERSITY, PITTSBURGH

Larry Hatch at his going-away party, August 23, 1956. CLAIRE MOORE

Isaly was driving home from a Pirates baseball game in 1961 when he swerved and hit a parked car. He was dead at 56 from a heart attack: The last of founder William Isaly's sons was gone.

Walter Paulo succeeded him in Youngstown as president, but it was Charles's son William R. Isaly who became the de facto leader: President of Marion, he succeeded Henry as president of Mansfield and Pittsburgh, and in Youngstown, he became chairman of the board and vice-president.

Henry's death came as supermarkets and fast foods were increasingly chipping away at Isaly's niche. Ron Campbell left his manager position in 1962: "They were opening stores slower than they were closing them, and we had very few shopping center locations. . . . As the supermarkets came and put in those nice deli and cheese departments, our business was being eroded." Then there was Dairy Queen: "They put a little building up on a piece of blacktop, and pretty soon they had your ice cream customers." There was also Dari-Delite (a division of Good Humor), Tastee-Freeze, and a thousand homegrown variations.

Isaly's Mansfield division tried reformatting its stores in 1962. General manager and Isaly relative Clarence Luedy announced that $800,000 would be spent constructing 12 "revolutionary" Swiss Dairy Stores—self-service groceries in chalet-style buildings—but two years later, only 3 Swiss stores had opened.

At the Highland Avenue Isaly's in New Castle, Bill and Wilma Belknap similarly removed their lunch counter and tables in 1965: "We enlarged it and made it a neighborhood convenience store," recalled Wilma. "Everything self-serve except the lunch meat department. We no longer made ice cream cones, milk shakes, sodas, or sundaes." An Isaly's without an ice cream counter was a telling sign for the chain.

Behind the counter at the Mt. Lebanon store are Ron Campbell (right, holding a Skyscraper) and Charles Isaly's son, John, at the deli case. John Isaly started at Pittsburgh's Mt. Lebanon store on New Year's Day, 1956. H. RON CAMPBELL.

Klondike production hadn't changed much in four decades: It was still a matter of freezing ice cream in a rectangular mold, then cutting into bars and dipping them in chocolate.

The process had become more mechanized, but the biggest change was the dropping of pink centers. H. William explained that pink ice cream "worked fine when most Klondikes were sold individually and over the counter. However, with improvement and wide use of home refrigerators, along with the introduction of Klondike multipacks, most bars were now being taken out and consumed at a later date. This made it impossible for the lucky winner to provide proof of his win to the store clerk. Therefore, the change from real pink center ice cream to "pink center" insert cards was made in the early '50s." Customers could even save their cards to get a whole six- or eight-pack. Party slices—vanilla bars with flavored shapes in the middle—continued to be made for holidays: cherry Valentine hearts, orange pumpkins, chocolate turkeys, and mint Christmas trees.

But mechanically inclined William R. knew of automated equipment that could be adapted to making bars. The "Polarmatic" was reconfigured to pour semisoft ice cream from a square nozzle, where a heated, rotating wire cut the flow into blocks. A conveyor carried them into a chill tower, and they'd emerge brick hard 11 minutes later. Chocolate was delivered in 82-degree tanks and poured over the ice cream (called enrobing).

A Polarmatic was installed at the Boulevard in 1961, making 75 Klondikes per minute. The Boulevard's old equipment was moved to Marion, while Youngstown continued putting its Klondikes on sticks.

Klondikes dry as they make their way down the turnscrew. Note the "lucky bar" slips at the bottom. The Polarmatic would make this process obsolete. GAYLORD LAMOND

Klondikes prepared for boxing. GAYLORD LAMOND

Pink Klondike Confessions

One of every 12 Klondikes had a lucky pink center (or stick or card), entitling the recipient to another free Klondike. But it seems there was a reason why it was so tough for a kid to get one. Bill Willmot, who started at Homestead, Pennsylvania, in 1940, remembered, "When Klondikes were delivered, one of the clerks would flick off a tiny piece of chocolate on one end of all of the Klondikes, looking for the pink centers. When they were found, they were stored separately in the freezer and sold to friends or pretty girls that we were trying to impress. The manager did not know about this practice, but what the heck, we were 16 and 17 years old."

Lester Lowery, who started at age 15 in the late 1930s at an Isaly's in McKeesport, remembered the pink-centered Klondikes, too: "I could sort of pull the paper back a little bit, and I could tell where the pink ones were. There were about six or seven layers of Klondikes in the can, and on each layer there would be one pink. I would pick some of them out and then hold them for when some of my friends would come in."

Despite new machinery, Isaly's slow decline continued. The Akron plant closed in 1963, and soon after, so did Canton. In Youngstown, 15,000 steel-related jobs had disappeared since World War II. Isaly's profits had held steady through 1959, when the branch made $600,000, but by 1963 profits had tumbled to $9,000. Youngstown's stores were deteriorating faster than Pittsburgh's, as most were older, but some also pointed to Walter Paulo's looser methods for not keeping up standards. Beaver Falls franchise owner Dean Bricker said, "Walter probably knew a lot, I'll give him that much credit, [but] he wasn't a great communicator. He tried to dominate, but he didn't have the personality to do that."

George Krohe said Paulo's gung-ho attitude that got things done also created friction: "Walter was the kind of guy, [when] they [needed to] put some piece of equipment in [the plant] and the engineers for the company told him that they'd have to move this particular wall to get this in and it would take so much time, Walter got a couple of his guys in that night and just took a couple sledgehammers and punched a hole in the wall and put the thing through. He says, 'There it is!' It was ragged and the cement was hanging loose, but that was Walter."

In April 1965, Walter Paulo was promoted to chairman of the board in Youngstown. William R. succeeded him as president, attorney Regis Gilboy succeeded him as secretary, and Richard S. Van Cleave succeeded Paulo as general manager. Van Cleave, a former executive vice-president of Bresler Dairy Enterprises of Chicago, assumed that title at Isaly's too.

Board members hailed Paulo's achievements, but some say that there were more than warm wishes behind his "promotion," especially as the chairman

was not recognized by the bylaws. Paulo's age wasn't a problem;
political office three years later. Declining sales were certainly ..
George Krohe and Art Frank thought his reassignment was retaliation ic.
ing the Columbus branch, where William R. was president, and for an earlic.
incident. "When W. R. was a youngster," explained Krohe, "Walter just didn't
like him, he just canned him, that's all, so when W. R. Isaly became president
of the company, he didn't like Walter, so he just canned *him*." Art Frank said
that by then, William R. "was powerful enough to get enough of the major
stockholders to stand with him."

Some Memorable Recipes from Isaly's

FROSTY FLIP
8 oz. sherbet ice cream (typically orange or rainbow)
1 oz. vanilla syrup
8 oz. carbonated water

Place 4 flat #24 scoops (2 oz. each) of sherbet into a 16-oz. milk shake
cup. Add vanilla syrup and carbonated water. Mix in milk shake machine
until ingredients form a heavy slush. Serve with a jumbo straw and soda
spoon. Yield: 1 serving.

BAKED BEANS
1 #10 can beans
1 pint water
1 1/2 cups brown sugar
2 cups tomato puree
1 tsp. grated onion
2 tsp. celery salt
2 tbsp. sweet liquor
2 strips bacon, diced fine
1 cup ketchup

Mix together and bake 30 minutes. Yield: 40 servings.

GRILLED WONDER PUPS
8 wieners
3 slices American cheese
4 slices bacon
1 cup barbeque sauce
1 cup water

Slit the wieners lengthwise. Cut each slice of cheese into 8 pieces. Put
3 pieces of cheese into the slits in each wiener. Cut the bacon in half and
wrap one piece around each wiener. Pour barbeque sauce and water over
the wieners. Bake uncovered in 400-degree oven for 20 minutes. Yield:
4 servings.

Paulo's office in the Youngstown plant had a 6-by-10-foot inventory room behind it. Upon his promotion, recalled Art Frank, he was relocated into that room: "I told him, 'Walter, I wouldn't give them the satisfaction of showing my face around here, I'd get the hell out.' So he stayed a year or so and then he went."

Van Cleave was the first outsider that Isaly's had brought in for a prominent position, which created a lot of ill will. Minerva store owner Bill Francis said of Paulo, "He gave us good products and good prices. They then hired a man [Van Cleave] who raised our prices and cheapened our product. . . . It was said that Isaly's had a million dollars in the bank when Paulo left, and when the new man's two-year contract was up, they were a million dollars in debt. The beginning of the end."

William R. also had his critics; George Krohe, among others, didn't like his management style: "He spent the first two years sitting in his office writing documents based on the AMA [American Management Association] out of New York. It wasn't that kind of company. . . . William R. joined the PAA [Pittsburgh Athletic Association] club in Pittsburgh and met other executives. . . . I have great respect for him, [but] he got carried away with himself."

H. William said William R. "was a pretty good business man. I mean, he had some real success with our company both with the Marion plant, and he had run a cheese plant and butter plant that we had out in Fort Wayne, so there was no reason to think that Bill couldn't do a good job. . . . He came to Pittsburgh and he did, for all intents and purposes, he did. He was a great guy, very business-minded, and he got himself into the business group out of New York that a lot of businessmen follow, got to their seminars and so forth. Bill started to go to these, and Bill sort of got caught up in some of these things, and he started to bring some of these programs and methods back and try to institute them into our family company." But he admitted, "Some of them didn't work very well." Changing ingrained procedures, no matter how necessary, would not be easy.

Immune Milk Mystery

A bit of mystery surrounds a special milk that Isaly's executive Walter Paulo championed. In fact, Paulo was a director and vice-president of Immune Milk Company of America in Cincinnati. Immune milk is prepared by injecting cows with antigens, and as such is regulated by the Food and Drug Administration.

Gerda Creelman attests that the stuff worked on her leg infection: "After two years of constant medical attention which proved unsuccessful, Dad . . . ordered the milk for me, and over a period of months, I drank two quarts of milk a day—one quart at a sitting. The milk, in a carton, had to remain frozen until the day one drank it. After a few months, the persistent bone infection cleared up. Following my positive experience, Dad mentioned it to a neighbor who had been a world traveler but who became crippled with arthritis and was bedridden. She, in turn, began drinking the milk and within a short period of time was out of bed, traveling again."

Checking the milk with Miss Ohio 1965 Valerie Lavin are Richard Van Cleave and William R. Isaly. GAYLORD LAMOND

A slew of other staff promotions followed, including Art Frank to general office manager, George Krohe to vice-president, and H. William's brother Tom Isaly to head of research and development.

Tom had married June Vaughan in 1960 and moved to Youngstown. Art Frank recalled, "I'll say this much for Tom, when the Pittsburgh fellows came up to try to help us out, naturally we resented it, and Tom was on the fence . . . but they did the best job they could with what they had to work with, and they treated people in Youngstown fairly. But they were the forerunners, shall we say, of the death knell."

In September 1965, Van Cleave announced the shuttering of the certified dairy farm, saying that the company didn't want to compete with its 350 suppliers. By the end of the month, Isaly's would have more than that bringing farmers' wrath. The front page of the *Pittsburgh Press* on September 30, 1965, screamed, "60 Pickets Arrested at Isaly's." That was only one of five mentions of the controversy that day. The strike was organized by the United Dairy Farmers (UDF), which claimed that its members received 8¢ per quart of milk but wanted 13¢. Isaly's Boulevard plant was randomly chosen for their protest.

William R. responded, "The Isaly Dairy Company has always purchased its milk from the Dairyman's Co-operative Sales Association at prices set and regulated by the Pennsylvania Milk Commission. . . . Our contract with DCSA and a Federal statute . . . prevent us from direct bargaining with dissident producer groups not represented by the DCSA." William R. said that Pennsylvania State University figures proved that they were paying 13¢ per quart to the DCSA: "The 5¢ difference is not our problem."

Pickets spread to Isaly's stores. Then the UDF filed a $13 million antitrust lawsuit against Isaly's, the DCSA, and three other dairies. The Teamsters

Police drag a farmer's wife from the Boulevard plant. The United Dairy Farmers protest began at midnight September 30, 1965, as hymn-singing pickets blocked trucks entering or leaving the Boulevard plant. Their numbers rose to about 400 by 4 A.M., but then began dwindling, as many had to return to their farms to milk their cows. Sixty pickets, including 13 women, were arrested around 9:00 A.M. when the farmers refused to break their lines so trucks could pass; it marked the first use of Pittsburgh's new police tactical unit, established for riot control. The city's safety director explained that because it was a demonstration and not a strike, the pickets were not allowed to block access to the property: "Never have we had any demonstrators so uncooperative or defiant of the law than the farmers." PITTSBURGH POST-GAZETTE

Union, however, called upon organized labor to ignore the UDF pickets, seeing it as an internal fight of DCSA.

Ohio farmers formed their own UDF chapter and began picketing the Youngstown plant with signs like, "We peasants haven't had a raise for 20 years and need more money to stay in business." But like in Pennsylvania, some UDF members were also DCSA members, even the Ohio UDF president.

"It cost us well over a million dollars," recalled Krohe. "They would do such dirty things. These farmers and farmers' wives would come in and say, 'Can I use your toilet facility?'. . . They'd slip down in the basement and they'd have the stink bomb or a skunk in a plastic bag, and rip it open and throw it back in the store."

The deadlock ended in April 1966 when the farmers agreed to remove the pickets and open negotiations, but the suit dragged on for years. UDF opened dozens of its own stores, a few still operating, but low prices remain a problem for dairy farmers.

Almost every Isaly's driver and production worker was in Local 205. Krohe said the stores were union, too: "We were the only ones that were union.

Shouldn't have happened, but it did. Put us at a disadvantage. We paid higher than our competitors, [and] towards the end, some of the people got more union oriented than company oriented, and that was always bad. They were working for the union, not the company."

. . .

John Isaly, who took over as Marion general manager in 1961, said the family had long talked of consolidating branches: "Everybody had their own ice cream carton, their own milk carton, and the economies of combining purchases weren't there, or having a unified direction as to what a store ought to even look like or be doing."

Isaly's wasn't alone; according to *The Great American Ice Cream Book* by Paul Dickson, "the 1960s proved to be the decade in which inefficient plants (many producing marvelous ice cream) and small companies died or were absorbed in droves. U.S. Department of Agriculture figures told of 1,656 plants closing between 1957 and 1969, and as the number of firms grew smaller, entities like Foremost, Beatrice Foods, and Sealtest grew bigger."

William R. recalled, "After my uncles died, we really didn't have good replacements, so it was a necessity to get [the branches] under one roof and have one direction. . . . The Ohio stores, particularly Youngstown, were very loose."

Art Frank agreed: "When they were getting started, almost anybody that would come in the office in Youngstown and say they had a storeroom in Timbuktu and they wanted to handle Isaly products . . . inside of three weeks there'd be an Isaly's sign up there and the truck would be on the route."

Consolidation couldn't solve every problem. As George Krohe said, "it takes an awful lot of white paint to make a bucket of black turn white." But Pittsburgh shareholders adopted a plan in December 1966, with 3,135 shares in favor and 1,209 against, and the other three branches followed suit.

The result was The Isaly Company, headquartered in Pittsburgh. One former Pittsburgh share converted into 56 shares of the new corporation, Youngstown into 21, Mansfield into 31, and Marion into 16. Great resentment grew from this, as some thought the exchange ratios favored Mansfield and Marion: older, smaller branches with fewer stores and lower sales.

"There were suspicions that somebody was going to do in the other," said Samuel's son Sam Isaly, by then a board member. "There were a variety of rather pained instances where you had to vote . . . and there is provision in the law in such instances for nonagreeing shareholders to cash out, and an important amount of shares were cashed out, and in particular, all the Pittsburgh shares were cashed out." As H. William remembered, "It just became nasty."

The announcement was made just after New Year's 1967: Under one umbrella were 365 dairy stores and 185 Ohio home delivery routes. The Marshall Creamery in Iowa was liquidated, and the four branches were renamed as divisions of The Isaly Company. A few days later, an article ran in Youngstown extolling Isaly's advancements but curiously ignoring the merger. Instead, it told of products under development, such as nonexpiring canned milk and low-low-calorie ice cream.

A month after the merger, H. William succeeded Richard Van Cleave as general manager of the Youngstown Division. Just a year earlier, directors had unanimously elected Van Cleave to the board, but now a letter to shareholders explained, "Our Manager in our Youngstown Division was not properly in control of that operation. It was further indicated that the results of this mismanagement had damaged our good name and image." Van Cleave became special staff assistant to the president.

Art Frank explained, "Youngstown was, I hate to say this, put under incapable managers. When they threw Walter out, they brought in this guy . . . R. S. Van Cleave. He never moved out of his office, he took care of it from his plush office, and they kept moving all of the Youngstown Division former supervisors and management people out of their jobs. . . . [Vice-president] Hershel [Rickard] quit. Gene Paulo, the plant superintendent, and myself were the only two that stayed. All the rest of the foremen quit, and these guys were mad at us, naturally. I said, 'Why should I quit? They're still giving me a check every payday, [though] they don't let me do anything. I just sit around.' And Gene Paulo said the same thing. We used to meet in the stockroom. We didn't have anything to *do*. When H. William Isaly came up, basically it was never admitted, but he was in charge of closing up the Youngstown plant. . . . He was in charge of getting rid of all these hot-shot experts they brought in."

H. William said that Youngstown "was just not doing well. Now, was that caused by the fact that Van Cleave was there for several years and wasn't really paying attention to it, or was it really caused by the fact that those old stores were really wearing out in Ohio faster than they were in Pennsylvania, people weren't getting home delivery anymore? I don't know. It's probably some of all of those things."

Four months into 1967, William R. sent a letter to stockholders: "Needless to say, consolidation within the newly merged company has not been free of problems and complications." Duplicate positions pitted supervisors against each other, and integrating the accounting proved so troublesome that it was postponed.

Sam Isaly remembered, "The merger was accomplishing de jure what had been operating de facto when the brothers were around, that it was operated as a unit even though the legal entities were separate. . . . Any problems of the combination were not business problems, they were emotional and family problems, and the business taken as a whole was in decline, and doing something about a legal structure wasn't going to change that."

Hopes were instead pinned on Isaly Shoppes. H. William said, "That was the younger of us saying this Isaly deal isn't going to work forever and we need to develop something new. . . . My brother Tom and my cousin John had gone and talked to W. R., and W. R. had enough vision to see that this was probably a pretty good deal."

The three made a trip in 1966 to observe similar chains: "We were really impressed with Friendly's," said John. "We started really beating the doors for that type of operation."

The Isaly Shoppe concept debuted at Allegheny Center Mall, Pittsburgh. GAYLORD LAMOND

H. William recalled, "We actually went around with their supervisors. What they didn't know is at the end of each day of visiting their stores, we would just simply go back to a hotel room, lock ourselves in, no drinks, and we would go over everything we had searched out that day and write it down."

The first Isaly Shoppe (they were called units, not stores) opened early in 1967 at Pittsburgh's Allegheny Center Mall. In May, William R. reported, "We feel we are very close to some important profit answers for our company." Another unit was under way near Youngstown University, featuring a colonial design of brick, paneling, Americana wallpaper, carriage lamps, and dark carpeting. There was table service but *no* dairy or ice cream cases.

The Shoppes proved Isaly's was finally catching up to such stalwarts as Howard Johnson's and Friendly's, though the company still wasn't building along highways. Even Eat'n Park had begun in 1952 to model its sit-down sections after coffee shops, which appealed to a similar customer but needed less land, smaller staffs, and had fewer "teen hangout" problems. Bob Moore, son-in-law of Larry Hatch and later Eat'n Park president, said the changes accelerated when McDonald's began stealing customers in the late '60s: "Eat'n Park had to decide: go with fast food, stay a drive-in, or change the image to a family restaurant—and that's what we did."

Isaly Shoppe menus showed photos such as the five-ounce Big Beef burger with pickles and chips for 65¢. Ice cream got more space than food: a Super Scooper of eight flavors with toppings, whipped cream, and a cherry was $1.35, and anyone who ate it all got a Super Scooper Super Man Award. But customers wondered why they couldn't get a cone.

In Marion, the first Shoppe opened in 1968. Division general manager John Isaly called the changes "so uniquely different that we have revised the name."

But looking back, he recalled, "There were those, I being one, that felt that the name ought to be something different so that there wasn't any confusion, that you walked in and you couldn't get chipped ham, bottled milk. The powers that be in Pittsburgh really wanted to continue to sell the chipped ham . . . so they felt the name could be retained, that the name Isaly Shoppe was different enough from the name Isaly's, which it isn't."

George Krohe, who now oversaw all 320 company stores, said, "The people were measuring us with the early days of the early Isaly's stores, and they'd come in and expect to get things at these very, very low prices, and it just wasn't working."

Two more Isaly Shoppes opened in Pittsburgh, and another was planned for the new Monroeville Mall. Krohe said, "I knew we were wrong with the Isaly Shoppe, and the guys from the mall . . . wanted to know in advance what's the name of this; they had to show it in their prospectus."

A name came to Krohe the morning he had to present it to the mall: "The founder of the company was William Isaly, and we're selling sweet products, so I thought Sweet William, and there was a little flower called sweet William. [H. William] was tryin' hard to get the name: Isaly Chariot, Isaly this, Isaly what-not. . . . And he said, 'Well, what is it, George?' I said, 'Call it Sweet William.' And there was no answer, no answer. And I thought, 'Oh hell, I blew that.' And all of a sudden he says, 'Oh, that's great! Go ahead!'"

H. William said, "This naming came soon after I was selected to be president, and I really took some guff from a lot of the board members, who said, 'You named that after you.' And of course I didn't. I wouldn't have even thought that it was me."

Krohe recalled, "About a week after we changed the name down in Bellevue from the Isaly Shoppe to Sweet William, I'm down there, same store, same everything . . . and there's a couple sittin' in the booth right next to me, and this guy said to his wife, 'Boy, you sure can tell the difference since this new outfit took over.' Ain't it funny!"

The Allegheny Center unit was revamped as a Sweet William, with Walter "Don" Jones as manager. He'd started with Isaly's in 1950 (marrying a coworker he'd tried to fire twice) and said because Sweet William was a new concept and division, "it was a leg up, supposed to be much classier." His best friend Bob Marchionda was made assistant manager at the Greentree unit.

In McKeesport, Thad Merriman adopted the Sweet William concept but not the name. When his 40-year-old Isaly's was razed for urban renewal, he opened The Canopy across the street with a deli up front and seating for 119. Ice cream came in mind-blowing servings, led by "The Canopy": 15 different scoops plus bananas, pineapples, hot fudge, marshmallows, pecans, and more.

At the nearby intersection of Routes 30 and 48, a Pig 'n Go restaurant had lasted only two months before defaulting on its rent. When Isaly's passed on the location for a Sweet William, landowner Hartley King opened it himself as King's Country Shoppe. Customers mistook it for a yard-goods store until for-mer Isaly's man Carl Benson joined up, helped the restaurant reorganize, and

Thad Merriman's White Oak, Pennsylvania, deli on Lincoln Way was remodeled in 1972 to sell self-service groceries. THAD MERRIMAN

changed its name to King's Family Restaurant. Benson said that King's emphasized its fancy desserts: "With Isaly's, they never went for anything real fancy. They tried to keep everything low cost and low priced, and I think one of their big problems was that they found it difficult to raise prices. . . . That was part of their undoing . . . forgetting people actually like to upgrade."

Another sign of changing times was the discontinuance of the Skyscraper in 1968. The scoop had evolved: Changes were made to the stem (straight versus angled), the length (long versus short), composition (hollow versus solid steel), and style (welded joint versus one piece). But Krohe said those couldn't compensate for industry changes: "People now buy ice cream that is five to eight degrees *above* zero. It had to be five to eight degrees *below* zero to cut it out straight. And then another thing happened—all the ice cream companies went to cardboard containers. Well, with [pointy scoops], you'd go through the side of the container."

H. William added, "You could not put a Skyscraper onto a sugar cone; you would break it. [But other stores] were all going to sugar cones, and that was by far and away the preference of American cone eaters. Second is everybody that had dip stores was doing single, double, triple dips in all different flavors, and with the Skyscraper, you could only do one scoop."

So H. William gathered as many scoops as he could wrestle off store owners and buried them, reportedly behind the Boulevard plant: "I've heard people say that they were dug up, but I don't believe it. And the reason people say that they're dug up is because everybody turns up with some scoops, but that's because everybody used to steal scoops and take them home."

Krohe said Henry Isaly had done the same thing in about 1960 when the angled-stem Skyscraper scoop came out: "We had several hundred of the old ones in our stockroom. This was a guarded secret . . . and they've never been found to this day."

Tom Isaly transferred back to Pittsburgh in 1968 to become director of purchasing for The Isaly Company. His son Phil was a regular at the Boulevard: "This was the family secret, and I was never allowed to say this, but the crunchies on the Klondikes are really Cracker Jacks. . . . We'd go down to the plant on the Boulevard of the Allies with my dad, and they would have the Cracker Jacks in these big bins, and all you had to do was lick your hand and stick it in the bin, and we'd sit there for an hour eating Cracker Jacks and getting sick as a dog, but we did it every Saturday."

• • •

By the end of 1968, Mansfield was closed, and Marion had stopped making ice cream. A few months later, Marion milk production ceased too; then its delivery routes were sold to Smith Dairy Products, which was opening Quick Chek convenience stores. Only its salesroom remained.

On April 4, 1969, The Isaly Company announced that H. William was succeeding William R. as president and treasurer. William R., who remained chairman of the board, had overseen the closing of about 100 stores during his seven-year reign—from 371 in 1962 to 270 in 1969.

H. William said, "We're going through this transition, and things aren't good, and finally the board of directors just voted that Bill should be replaced. I'm not sure that they were really fair about that. I mean, they just didn't like what was happening, especially from a profit standpoint, so they look around and they say, 'Well, who do we have to put in here?' Well, there wasn't much to put in there, so they put me in there. A lot had grown to hate W. R., and frankly, he didn't deserve it. . . . I thought generally he handled it pretty well and he was a good businessman. He used the law firm of Thorp Reed & Armstrong, and he was guided every step of the way by what they told him. Thorp Reed & Armstrong, in my opinion, was the best law firm in Pittsburgh. He did everything right, but it made all these people mad."

With Marion closed, William R.'s brother John Isaly said, "I got disenchanted with the direction, or lack of direction." He left for Buxton's Country Shops of Jamesburg, New Jersey, one of the companies he'd seen while prospecting the Isaly Shoppe idea. Interestingly, Hartley King, of King's Country Shoppe, knew company founder John Buxton and had also visited with Carl Benson to gather ideas. King recalled that the up-and-coming ice cream restaurants all had a similar look because they were being outfitted by a company called Grand Rapids. King approached that outfitter too, but said, "When Isaly's got wind of it, they told Grand Rapids, 'You won't do ours,' so I had it done locally." Isaly's also turned King down when he was looking for a firm to make ice cream for him: Isaly's was in no mood to help a competitor to their one glimmer of hope, Sweet Williams. Three decades later, King's indeed has grown to 35 locations and 17 flavors of Hartley's Choice ice cream.

Youngstown had finally gotten a Polarmatic to automate Klondike production in early 1969, but that September, H. William announced that Youngstown's ice cream production would cease, "to improve efficiency by moving all ice cream production to Pittsburgh." He said that the company was also "tightening" the area served by the plant—closing all 14 Cleveland Isaly's, all 8 in Columbus, and 30 of 195 in Youngstown—but that no further contraction was likely.

Ron Totin, former West View owner, said that the company was noticeably slipping: "I hate to say this, but I seen it starting as far back as 1968. I mentioned to the supervisors at the time, around Meadville there was a convenience chain up there called Red Barn. . . . When I came back from the service [in 1963], Stop-N-Go was in the area. I think this is where we missed the boat."

But Isaly's directors had enough; a December 11, 1969, letter to shareholders noted, "the company continues to suffer substantial operating losses . . . [so] management, at the Board's direction, has been seeking out potential buyers of your stock or a merger partner."

H. William recalled, "My job for at least half of the time I was president was to find a buyer, and I delayed, put it off, until finally one meeting, the board just said, 'You either get us a buyer, or we're going to put somebody in your position to do it.'"

June Isaly recalled, "My husband [Tom] tried to get some of the younger Isalys to try to buy up that stock so that it would remain in the family. . . . I always thought that was a major part of his heart problem, when they sold. It just was no longer family, and it was real hard to let that go."

A tentative sale was negotiated for the Murray Holding Company (MHC) to pay $4.58 per share, with an additional $4.58 later. The holding company would use the cash assets of the company to cover its $2.4 million investment.

This brought an immediate response from a self-styled "hard-core minority group." One of them was Walter Paulo, who'd been elected to the first of three terms as state representative in 1968, at age 66. The others were former company vice-president Hershel Rickard and William E. Isaly, a great-nephew of William Isaly who'd revitalized Cleveland's stores in 1965 and was still Youngstown salesroom manager. Their letter to stockholders noted that "you are being paid for the stock with your Isaly Company money." They put forth their own idea: "The company could pay a dividend of $1.00 in December and another $1.00 in January. They have the extra funds." A follow-up letter enumerated their complaints, among them that shareholder equity was over $17 a share, versus the $9.16 offer. But the value was surely dropping: 1969 saw a $952,000 loss, double that of 1968.

The Youngstown plant was being emptied in anticipation of the closing of all Ohio operations. On January 10, 1970, Paulo announced that stockholders and employees hoped to purchase the plant and had blocked the sale to MHC.

While directors "seem to be interested only in getting their money and going home," he said, "Isaly blood" had "rounded up sufficient cash" for the purchase.

H. William said, "Whenever a company is sort of in trouble . . . you'll always get the old guard wanting to say, 'Hey, let's all buy it.' . . . We were simply closing up one of the plant facilities, because by then, it was merged into The Isaly Company. . . . Pittsburgh was the stronger of the companies, and I would say that was mostly due to my dad, frankly. And unfortunately, the loss of strength in Youngstown was caused by the death of Samuel Isaly at a very early age. Samuel Isaly—that's young Sam's father—my dad used to call him a real visionary businessman, maybe best of all the Isalys. . . . Sam [Jr.] has inherited some of that."

In fact, Sam Isaly sent a letter to shareholders on January 23, 1970, explaining his research into the holding company's proposal, including a review by three investment banking houses, all of which, he claimed, "felt it was an unprecedented attempt to steal a company for nothing."

Despite some profits in Ohio, the Youngstown plant closed that summer. A terse letter sent to its stores shows how much Isaly's had strayed: "Due to changes in our production and delivery system, it will be impossible to make deliveries in your area. This 30-day notice should allow you plenty of time to arrange for new suppliers. As of June 30, 1970, we request that you remove all signs and advertising displaying the Isaly name."

Art Frank was told to liquidate the 70 Ohio stores: "They were neighborhood dairy stores doing $100 a day maybe in business . . . and I told them, 'I wouldn't sell to my worst enemy any of those that I had left—close them,' and that's what they did. The stores that I had the guys take over, some of 'em bought it for $2,000, $3,000. It was ridiculous." For those, "Pittsburgh tried to [collect] a franchise fee . . . of so much a month, and if they didn't pay it, the sign had to come down. . . . I said, 'Tell them if they want the sign down, it's all right. Tell them to come and take it down.' They never took the signs down."

There was at least one happy note for Art Frank: He was able to buy the Isaly Chalet at Canfield Fairgrounds, where he'd helped since 1935. He and his family ran it until 1985.

The Marion salesroom had to close, too, as the trip from Pittsburgh

Art Frank, left, at the Canfield Fairgrounds stand, which really looked like a chalet. Art started helping in 1935; without a way to lock it, he'd often sleep there overnight. His daughter Phyllis Pellin grew up at the plant and the Chalet and often went with her dad to audit and inventory stores. "Isaly's was a family back then. I received a lot of valuable life lessons. . . . Isaly's—great memories— my family." ART FRANK AND PHYLLIS PELLIN

would be too long. The abandoned plant was reduced to serving as a haunted house at Halloween. Angelo Doria recalled, "It took a while for it to sink in. First job at age 17, and 27 years later, out of a job at age 43. Took a while to get over it. . . . The hardest deal after 27 years at Isaly's was my severance pay. Total of two weeks' pay, which I thought was a low blow."

John Isaly had just returned to Marion, as Buxton's was struggling, like Isaly's. He and his wife reopened the Isaly Shoppe independently, and within half a year, they were expanding.

In August 1970, The Isaly Company announced that it was not "running to the hills," just closing stores that no longer met standards. The unnamed spokesman said they would open new stores when better locations were found, but the company, meanwhile, was liquidating its remaining subsidiaries: Mid-Ohio Realty Company, Idee Oil Company, the New Wilmington Cheese Company and Swiss Maid Stores, which oversaw Mansfield's Swiss Dairy Stores.

Sam Isaly made a bid for the company in 1971, offering $13.50 a share, but board chairman John Martig III felt that it was too low. He suggested $15 a share, but Sam never offered again. Krohe said Martig "was bright . . . but he was a banker, basically, and he thought everything would run the same as a bank for him. It isn't quite that way when you're making ice cream cones."

In March 1972, Martig announced an offer to purchase Isaly's for $6.5 million ($26 million today) by the joint group of Venture Capital Funds of Cumberland Associates and E. M. Warburg, Pincus & Company, Inc. Though their $14.30 a share offer was less than the $16 originally discussed with the group, Martig seemed relieved that a cash deal could be completed within 90 days.

H. William said stockholders seemed satisfied: "They shouldn't have been, but they were. [The board] wanted it sold, and the buyer knew it. I can remember some of the last negotiating meetings with the board. They talked tough in the beginning, but they crumbled. . . . [B]ut my job was to find a buyer, and I did."

H. William was succeeded as president by Gaylord LaMond, head of food development at Federated Department Stores, Inc., and former president (and savior) of the Chock Full O' Nuts fast-food chain. He recalled, "I was president of a shell corporation at Federated Department Stores looking at acquisitions around the country, and Isaly's at that time, it didn't fit into the Federated image. About the only one at Federated who was interested was Mr. Fred Lazarus, one of the founders, [but] it didn't have the glamour. [Isaly's] had hidden assets, but the business wasn't producing any bottom-line results. . . . They hadn't really done much as far as bringing new product lines into the stores to excite customer interest. They clung to the old production, and some of those things had to be traded up. And then the Klondike, which was probably one of the biggest assets they had, they hadn't done anything to market it." Isaly's sold 10 million Klondikes a year, making the non-labor-intensive bar attractive as revenues were plunging.

H. William said LaMond was "very involved and active, and very good. . . . I think Gaylord didn't hesitate to close stores. [H]e pretty well let me alone, because he didn't understand the dairy plant, so I really ran the dairy plant, did the negoti-

Gaylord LaMond and H. William Isaly celebrate the purchase of The Isaly Company by LaMond and his investors. PITTSBURGH POST-GAZETTE

ating, and I had some involvement with the Sweet Williams [with] my brother Tom."

LaMond said, "During the first year, it was somewhat of a struggle, but then we got things turned around . . . upgrading the stores, cleaning them up, putting some new equipment in, and we built some new Sweet Williams, because the Sweet Williams had more of an opportunity for volume than the Isaly's." New units opened in 1974 at Fort Steuben Mall, Ohio; in 1975 in Shenango Mall near New Castle, Pennsylvania; and in 1977 in Southland Shopping Center in Pleasant Hills, Pennsylvania.

But Don Jones, who became a Sweet William supervisor in 1973, said, "When Gaylord LaMond bought them, he just put [Sweet Williams] anywhere there was a lease available. Whether it was a good location or not, he built one. He just wanted to grow in numbers." George Krohe agreed: "When Gaylord and his gang got in, they didn't give a damn as long as somebody paid them a franchise fee and bought stuff from them."

Krohe said that LaMond was "always very gentle and kind," but "he lowered our standards in quality." He recalled a taste-test meeting: "Gaylord was standing beside me, and there was something, I tried it and I said, 'I pick this.' . . . 'Oh no,' he says, 'this is like 1,000 percent better.' I said, 'Gaylord, you asked me what I like, and I like this. If you don't want my opinion, don't invite me anymore." Krohe laughed: "I never got invited again. Because I spoke the truth, and he knew it."

But LaMond said he was battling waste and neglect: "I probably spent as much time visiting stores, talking with employees and managers, and going with the supervisors to each and every store. . . . A number of the stores had, I don't want to say, gone in disrepair, but they hadn't been [kept up], and in this business you gotta keep spending a buck."

To some employees, the stores were still viable. Mary Jo (Torek) Chiodo, who worked at a Homestead, Pennsylvania, Isaly's, said, "We served a full menu. . . . A small-town atmosphere abounded." But most employees remember these years differently. Plant manager Paul Clever said Henry Isaly had told him, "Your job is here anytime, forever." But in 1974, Clever was forced to retire when he turned 65.

Art Frank had a similar story: In 1975, after 40 years with Isaly's, he was called to a meeting in a parking lot. As he suspected, he was given a paper to sign saying that he had resigned—and they wanted his company car on the spot, 60 miles from home. Art balked: He wanted termination with full benefits, and said that he'd keep the car until he got a new one. So he drove home: "I told

Klondike Wrappers

Klondikes were originally bagged in glassine, but eventually foil was used, like Eskimo Pie. Klondikes' wax-laminated foil wrappers have long featured a pebble embossing, not only to add shimmer but also to soften the foil for wrapping in a dead fold, which allows it to be opened without tearing. The polar bear image has been used as long as anyone can remember, but the current-style bear was instituted by H. William Isaly in the early 1970s.

my wife what happened. She said, 'Wonderful, wonderful! Maybe now you'll sleep at night.'"

But by 1977, there were rumors that Isaly's was again for sale. "A lot of us anticipated that," recalled H. William. "If venture-capital money was in there, we knew the program: They buy a turnaround company, they have it for five or seven years, and then they sell it. . . . Gaylord fell in love with the company just like everybody does and would've loved to stay there, but I think the pressure really came then from his venture-capital people, who said, 'We're ready to turn around and sell this.'"

Franchisees received a letter from LaMond in April stating that Isaly's was "merging" with "a larger organization, thus giving us access to additional sources of capital and enabling us to expand much more rapidly. . . . Isaly's is now a subsidiary of Clabir Corporation."

Clabir, based in Greenwich, Connecticut, was headed by Henry D. Clarke Jr., a Pittsburgh native whose family owned about two-thirds of its over-the-counter stock. It oversaw 6 dry cleaners, 8 Taco Bells, 12 Long John Silvers, and 8 Four 'n 20 Pie Restaurants. Clabir also had industrial interests, leading to the main complaint still voiced by Isaly's faithful—that subsidiary Flinchbaugh manufactured antitank missiles near York, Pennsylvania. Clarke heard the missile complaints but said, "Let me assure you, I always knew a hell of a lot more about the ice cream business than I did the artillery business."

The $7.3 million purchase included 29 Sweet Williams, 62 delis, and 81 franchises. Clabir Food Services consolidated in Pittsburgh under Isaly's management, with LaMond as president and chief executive officer. Tom Isaly quit to pursue restaurant design, but like his father and uncles, he would pass away young due to heart problems. His tombstone is engraved with a Skyscraper cone.

At Clabir's first annual meeting after buying Isaly's, Clarke credited LaMond with managing Clabir Food Services into the black. Probably few noticed, however, when LaMond stated that the "food operation could grow out of its present headquarters at the Isaly plant."

Going National, Staying Local

FOR ITS FIRST MOVE, CLABIR ANNOUNCED THAT IT WOULD CONVERT SIX FOUR 'n 20 Pie Restaurants in New York City into Sweet Williams. The first reopened April 1, 1978, but weeks later, all the locations were sold.

"We made the decision," recalled Gaylord LaMond, "with Taco Bells out in California, that we'd be better off to sell those to the management out there because of the cost of going back and forth out there, and the same thing with the Long John Silvers in Connecticut, and New York had the Four 'n 20 Pies."

Instead, H. William was directed to find a plant for making Klondikes near East Coast markets. He chose the 1922-built Bupp's Dairy for $135,000 in Hanover, Pennsylvania; the Hanover Klondike Company opened in May 1978 with H. William as president. The entire production line was on the first floor and as straight as possible for faster speeds and fewer damaged bars. By summer, production hit 7,000 bars per hour.

With Hanover open, H. William said, "we went to Philadelphia to see if we could get some stores to carry Klondikes. They laughed at the product. They said it was too big, too expensive. We finally talked a couple of the major chains into taking the product." Twelve weeks of TV commercials of a bear and a prospector advertised "the bear-size bar with the big rich taste." Newspaper ads also ran, with a contest offering the winner a choice of a $2,000 gold bar or a trip for two to the Klondike region. Klondike quickly captured 4 percent of Philadelphia's ice cream market.

"Once we had the Klondike plant in Hanover," said H. William, "that enabled [Clarke] to close the Pittsburgh plant . . . and we farmed out the [bulk] ice cream business."

Henry Clarke watches Klondikes roll by at the Clearwater plant. BILL WAX

Gaylord LaMond remembered, "At the Boulevard plant, a lot of the equipment was from the 1930s, approaching 45 years in age, and they kept repairing it. . . . When the plant was finally closed, there was an awful lot of equipment that went begging. Junk dealers would pick it up because no one else in the industry would want it, and in the food industry, your growth and profitability are dependent on technological advances, not living in the past."

Clarke said then, "The building is multistory, and this makes material handling very inefficient. Our hardening space for ice cream is very limited and restricts good, efficient production runs. In general, we can no longer produce ice cream as economically or as cheaply as we can buy it."

Clarke also pointed to another factor: "Why did we do what we did? And it's one word, the Teamsters. The head of the union . . . did some wonderful things like punch our personnel manager in the nose; he stormed out of an arbitration meeting after I think he had lost two meetings, screaming he was going to get us."

Plant worker Peter Argentine recalled, "The saddest day of my life was when Isaly Dairy closed up. I had days of mourning and bereavement. Some people even took sick they were so depressed; they just couldn't adjust to the fact that they closed up." Company headquarters remained at the plant, but 75 workers and drivers were cut.

Manager Ron Kragnes (left) and employees celebrate the first Four 'n 20 Pie Restaurant to be converted to a Sweet William in Brooklyn, 1978. Though six conversions were planned, this was apparently the only one completed, and it closed soon after. GAYLORD LAMOND

That's a Lot of Ice Cream!

The first ice cream factory opened in 1852, and by 1859, the United States was producing 4,000 gallons of ice cream a year. By 1899, production exceeded 5 million gallons. Advances in equipment and technology helped the industry keep expanding. When the depression hit, annual production was about 300 million gallons a year. But ice cream recovered. By the early 1960s, output had reached 1 billion gallons a year, and by the 1990s, it topped 1.5 billion.

Sources: K. A. Hyde and J. Rothwell, *Ice Cream* (Edinburgh: Churchill Livingston, 1973); A. C. Baer, *The Preparation and Processing of Ice Cream Mix* (Milwaukee: Olsen, 1927); U.S. Department of Agriculture.

Isaly's decision to farm its bulk ice cream to the lowest bidder showed; in a 1979 survey of 11 ice creams, *Pittsburgh* magazine ranked Isaly's tenth (beating only United Dairy Farmers), calling it, "[t]oo sweet, with a rubbery texture and the aftertaste of the cardboard carton container. Bits of other ice cream in the scoop. . . . Signs say: 'I remember Isaly's.' We remember it better."

Krohe said that closing the Boulevard was a big blow: "That's the beginning of the end: We didn't have Isaly products. You can only fool some of the people some of the time, and the products were not what people knew as Isaly's. . . . The children coming up weren't brought up in Isaly stores, and they weren't gonna buy something just because it had the name Isaly on it. . . . [Clabir] forgot that quality is the key word."

Clarke admitted, "I decided we would focus on novelties, and that ended up being a mistake. . . . If you were to go to [Hanover] you would see a beautiful big cold store, and you would see 23 acres that was laid out to build an ice cream factory, not just for Klondikes but bulk ice cream, and if you look closely at the 13 acres we had out in California, you would see that there was room for a bulk ice cream operation." But expanding the Klondike took precedence.

Sweet Williams also seemed poised for growth: There were 29, and when a new one opened in Reading, Pennsylvania, it surpassed the sales forecast by 50 percent. "We redeveloped the concept, added a bakery," recalled Clarke, "but even with the money we spent, we couldn't really make it into a concept that seemed to be competitive enough to build a hundred of them."

Former Sweet William supervisor Bob Marchionda remembered it differently: "Clabir destroyed [Isaly's] image so bad. . . . The only salvation we thought was the Sweet William, but then they were so rundown at that point, we kept them together with paper clips. . . . no remodeling money, no repairs, no nothing." Supervisor Harry Larabee left in 1979: "When Henry Clarke bought it, why he was only interested in the bottom line. I left then. I couldn't put up with his shenanigans. He wanted to cut the quality of the products and make a higher gross, and I said no way, and so I left."

Bob Marchionda (left) and Don Jones worked together for years at Isaly's. Here, they man the Sweet William at 5th and Liberty in Pittsburgh about 1979. DON JONES

Clarke said that's because his affections were with Klondike: "I remember telling Bill Isaly . . . to make sure that no matter how fast we start making this, and no matter how many places we take them or wherever we make them, that they are going to taste like a Klondike. We need to cut the cost of it so we can do more advertising, but you have my approval to stop the plant, stop anything you want to do if we're not making the Klondikes the way they taste. [Isaly's] never saw any reason to reduce the size, reduce the quality of the chocolate, to change the ice cream, to stop the dead-fold wrap, which made it look like it was hand wrapped, and to do all those things. While everybody, Eskimo Pie and so forth, was putting fake ice cream [ice milk], paraffin in their chocolate, shrinking their size and doing a variety of things, the Isaly family stuck to what they did."

A second line added in 1979 boosted Hanover's capacity to 60 million Klondikes a year (compared with the Boulevard's 11 million) and paved the way for entering Florida: "It was a thousand miles away, which wasn't great," said Clarke, "but Hanover has a lot of distribution companies located there, because if you look at a map, it's very well situated."

Isaly's celebrated its fiftieth anniversary in 1979, though previous anniversaries had celebrated the Boulevard's 1931 opening, not its 1929 incorporation. Plans were laid in 1978 with the ordering of new Skyscraper scoops. Then came the series of ads headlined "I remember Isaly's." Local TV and movie celebrity Rege Cordic offered recollections like, "I'm hamming it up for the hometown." A commemorative 15-foot cone was built at Kennywood Park using one ton of vanilla ice cream.

When four Isaly's stores applied for liquor licenses, the company called it a test for making a comeback in its golden anniversary. Stores were now selling cigarettes across the counter, and 15 had instant photo processors. These were no longer the Isaly's of Larry Hatch.

Klondike, meanwhile, did so well in Florida that it was expanded into Connecticut, New York, Maryland, Virginia, North and South Carolina, and Georgia. The key to its rapid expansion was using food brokers who worked on commission to get products into stores.

But Isaly's bottom line still sagged: 1980 losses totaled $2.4 million. Clabir's annual report blamed the downturn on the gas shortage, changing traffic patterns, supermarket delis, "and a substantial increase in the number of competitor-owned convenience stores." Twenty-seven Isaly's were closed, and the Boulevard was sold to Presbyterian-University Hospital for $3.3 million (though the Isaly's salesroom remained).

Two more transactions were set to bring another $3 million. Isaly Company president and CEO Robert Scrivener stepped down to purchase six Sweet Williams, while Delicatessen Distributing Inc. (DDI) was negotiating to buy the delis. DDI, operated by James Deily, was a food distributor that supplied Isaly's stores. But both deals fell through. Deily's son Jay remembered, "We decided to graciously back out because we had some concerns with some areas with the company. . . . There was a period when pensions were a big concern and as to how things were set up, funded."

The 28 stores and 70 licensees were finally sold in 1981 to Custom Management Corporation (CMC) of Wilkes Barre, Pennsylvania, an operator of 300 food service contracts in 18 states and some casual restaurants. The Isaly's trademark remained with Clabir, but in essence, there were now two Isaly companies: the Klondike maker and the delis.

So What *Is* Chipped Ham?

The chipped part is easy—that's just the thin slicing. The real question is, What is the chopped ham that's used for chipping? A 1983 article by Pat Kiger in *Pittsburgh* magazine explained the manufacturing process: "Out of a 100-pound hog, somewhere between 15 and 20 pounds end up as chipped ham. . . . A hog leg which will become a conventional ham is trimmed into the familiar football shape, and the fat and muscle trimmings are collected, placed in a special machine, and tumbled to separate the protein (which, when the meat is reshaped, will act as a binding agent). While the meat is in the machine, seasonings are also added. The resulting mixture, which resembles a sort of flesh-colored pudding, is put into a paper-lined metal can (which molds it into a loaf) and cooked for 5½ hours. . . . The finished product contains about 17 percent fat."

"We didn't really buy the company with the idea that we saw a deli store on every corner in America," said Clarke. "We would have had to go much heavier into the grocery business. That's a nice thing to say, but it doesn't make any sense. . . . We thought Sweet William was the thing to expand, so we worked on that for about a year and a half, and when that didn't work, we just decided that we were Klondike." It was no help to the delis that the steel towns that once fueled Isaly's growth were now struggling with layoffs and mill closings.

CMC president and CEO John C. Metz was also a Pittsburgh native who had once worked at Isaly's. "We're going to put the quality of Isaly back into the name," he said then; plus, Isaly's was a way "to diversify into the commercial business." CMC formed a subsidiary, Custom Restaurant Corporation (CRC), to oversee Isaly's. Metz planned to immediately spend half a million dollars revamping the stores. Closed Isaly's were reopened as "Isaly's Eats and Sweets," and a store even opened to the east in Harrisburg's Capitol Complex.

Metz said at the time, "The delis never caused financial trouble. They've always been a profitable part of the chain. . . . When Clabir got into the Sweet William shops and the manufacturing of Klondikes, that's when they got into trouble." But a half year later, Metz purchased the 16 Sweet Williams for $3.5 million; two were refashioned immediately as Eats and Sweets. CMC director

John Metz chips ham for his new creation, the Big I. BOB MARCHIONDA

of operations Jack Donohue announced, "In the past there was apprehension because Clabir closed a lot of stores. Isaly's is now doing a complete reversal, because CMC is looking for new places to open. There's a positive feeling about it all. It's exciting."

Not everyone agreed that things were improving. Longtime Isaly's man Archie Mitchell and his wife Lou bought the Etna, Pennsylvania, Isaly's in 1980. Lou said that problems started in 1982, when "Jack Donohue came from CMC and said, 'Give us $4,000 or drop the Isaly name.'" Instead they changed the name to Mitchell's Deli. Longtime employee Margie DeArmit said it was more than a question of money: "When Custom took over, they came in and said if you want to stay, reapply for your job and start over [for tenure and pension]. That's no way to treat a human being."

Klondike sales had risen to $15 million a year, and market shares were amazing—55 percent in Dallas, 65 percent in New York City. One reason was that there were no national competitors, though there were 20-some regional bars, including Eskimo Pie's Penguin Bar, Vroman's Gold Rush Bar, Pierre's Block Buster, Sealtest's Polar B'ar, and Superior Dairy's Yukon Bar. Isaly's brought suit against Superior for "stealing the image" of Klondike by picturing polar bears on a silver-blue arctic wrapper, and the company was forced to change its design.

The Isaly Company also started proceedings in 1982 against Kraft Foods' Sealtest division for marketing the Polar B'ar, again for packaging that was too similar. Henry Clarke said Sealtest distributed Klondike in Florida, but when the head of Sealtest wanted to expand distribution, Clarke said no: "So subsequent court depositions say that he left that meeting and went out and basically a week later brought in his people and said, 'All right, we gotta create a Klondike.' . . . It took us seven years and two trips to the Supreme Court, but we finally won $8.5 million."

The Isaly Company (i.e., Klondike) lost almost another $1 million in 1981 but continued expanding. With sales outstripping production—even with bars being made under contract—a second plant was built in Clearwater, Florida, which tripled production. H. William relocated there: "I was the purchaser, I was in charge of quality control, I was in charge of new lines, in charge of storage and shipping, and so it sounds like I was running the whole company, but I wasn't. But I was in charge of things that had directly to do with the quality of that Klondike bar."

Plans were announced for a chocolate ice cream Klondike, as well as ice cream slices, Yukon Yogurt, fancy desserts, and pies. In fact, a third plant was already being planned for California, and by 1984, Klondike was in 40 states and became the first ice cream brand to have a multimillion-dollar national TV campaign. Six 30-second ads had actors perform antics to the jingle, "What would you do for a Klondike bar?" Still, the $5 million spent on marketing in 1984 only caused net earnings to dip. Undaunted, Clarke pursued test marketing the Klondike in England: "We spent a lot of time working with the Irish government to build a factory at Waterford . . . but I just couldn't bring myself to let somebody else produce the Klondike."

CMC, meanwhile, had tried to revitalize the delis with new products and promotions: Isaly's chocolates, the Isaly Chipper (ice cream between two chocolate chip cookies), ads on buses, sponsorship of Pittsburgh Steelers broadcasts, the two-foot-long Super Steeler Hoagie, the Tailgater package (hot entrees, cold salads, a dozen side dishes, and plasticware), E. T. Sundaes (named for the movie), even monthly Extra Buck Awards for managers. But they didn't work.

Don Jones had risen to director of operations when he was called to a meeting with five other supervisors, including Bob Marchionda and Jack Donohue. The meeting was short: "As of today, we no longer need your services."

Jones says that Metz, who wasn't at the meeting, "decided he was gonna make one operation, which was the institutional, take over the retail so that the supervisors and district managers from the institutional end took our jobs. . . . I did have some good times, but I also have some bitter feelings because of being let go with 33 years of service."

Marchionda said of Metz, "The sad part about it, he had a genuine concern. He made a genuine attempt to resurrect a dying business." Marchionda was asked to stay and run the Greentree restaurant, but without his company car and credit cards. He stayed: "Even though John Metz pulled the trigger and wasted a lot of my friends . . . he just got stuck in a no-win situation. When the time came, he had to pull the plug on everybody, or he'd have lost his investments. You don't like what happened, but you can justify what happened with Metz, but with Clabir, you just can't. There's a bitter pill in my mouth, and it'll always be there."

Franchisee Mohammed Saleem decided to sell his Isaly's: "When we bought out the five stores, supervisor Jack Donohue used to work for Isaly's company; he did good. But Custom Restaurant let everybody go. What happened was Custom Restaurant Corporation didn't know how to run Isaly's operation. Actually, that's the truth; they were in a hospital cafeteria operation, and Isaly's is a family type of operation."

"Custom Management," whispered George Krohe, "didn't do a good job of it. . . . Sure, a lot of things had changed, and maybe we didn't change fast enough, but there was always a depth of management there. . . . They figured, 'well, we'll do it our way. Hell, it goes, we can make it go.' . . . I remember a remark that was made by one of the men who . . . was gonna change things around, and he was told, 'That won't work, we're gonna lose business, we're gonna lose customers.' And he said, 'Eh, lose customers—we'll get new customers.' You don't do that. You hold your old customers, and then you get new ones."

John Metz said that when he bought the chain, "I looked at it more as a heart decision than as a business decision. We worked hard to upgrade and renovate the stores. No one had put any money in the stores. They were tremendously let go. It was already starting to slide in sales before we went in." With customers streaming to the suburbs and Klondikes available in every supermarket, Metz called James Deily of DDI and offered him the stores.

CMC had purchased 28 stores and 70 licensees in 1981; three years later, it sold 14 stores and about 40 licensees to DDI. Metz kept the Sweet Williams to sell off individually or convert to J. Clark's restaurants, named for himself, John Clark Metz.

DDI's connection to Isaly's stretched back to the 1950s, when James Deily was sales manager for Oswald & Hess, a meat processor that supplied Isaly's.

When the Boulevard store closed in 1984, George Aston had been with Isaly's 40 years, Delores Bluemle for 35. The New York Times *noted, "to hear the mourners talk, no one would know that others, still open, are scattered through Pittsburgh and its suburbs." Aston said the troubles began when the plant closed: "The ice cream was really never the same after that, and the customers knew it. Business started falling off." It took only a week for landlord Presbyterian Hospital to announce that it was opening its own Old Ice Cream Works, featuring chipped ham, Klondikes, and "mile-high cones" in a 1950s setting. A hospital spokesman said the expected $150,000 yearly profit would help "the hospital to reduce costs. . . . It's an innovative approach to reducing the cost of health care." Nine months later, the Works closed, and Delicatessen Distributing Inc., reopened it as an Isaly's.* PITTSBURGH POST-GAZETTE

He also owned Indian Coffee, makers of Isaly's Boulevard brand, then purchased Breakfast Cheer. His Campbell & Woods brand went to McDonald's, Winky's, Eat'n Park, and cafeterias. Jay Deily recalled, "We brought the bags of green beans off the piers in New York on a daily basis. . . . We were the largest coffee roaster between New York and Chicago." Deily also acquired Fried Provision Company, a processor of lunch meats (such as Fort Pitt brand) that Isaly's used. In 1978, he set up DDI and began distributing for Isaly's too. When DDI bought the delis, it found a ready-made general manager—Jack Donohue, released from CMC a year earlier.

Clabir also tried selling The Isaly Company but gave up after four months, instead diversifying its holdings as a way to raise funds. It wasn't uncommon—even the old Isaly companies had had multiple investments through treasury bills, stocks, and bonds—but this was on a much grander scale. The Isaly board issued 4 million shares of stock to Clabir in exchange for Clabir's holdings in two British companies: Steaua Romana PLC, a developer of oil and gas properties, and Sheraton Securities International PLC, a commercial property developer. The Isaly Company name was changed to AmBrit, Inc., to reflect its American and British holdings; Isaly Klondike became a division.

• • •

Flush with money, Isaly Klondike expansions surged ahead. In 1985, the California plant opened east of Los Angeles in Rancho Cucamonga. The Clearwater plant added a second line too, so that the three plants were making 1.2 million Klondikes *daily*, up from the Boulevard's 150,000.

Advertising and promotion were increased to $10.3 million in 1986, but sometimes the promotions worked too well; Clarke recalled, "we used to run out, and we had what we called the 'phantom truck.' We would tell five different people that a truck was on the way, but unfortunately, it was only one truck."

The product line had grown to include Klondike Nuggets, 15 bite-size bars to a box, and ice cream sandwiches with the Klondike logo on the wafer. AmBrit had also gone on a buying spree, purchasing Wilbur Chocolate for $42 million cash, then Popsicle Canada (including 24 plants) for $28 million. But the end of the 1987 fiscal year saw AmBrit with a $3.7 million loss, mostly from the British holdings acquired to infuse Klondike with operating funds. Then late in 1988, the Isaly president and CEO resigned.

AmBrit's 1989 annual report began optimistically, but further down was the truth: The company had missed some interest payments and dividends. "As a result," the report stated, "holders of the Clabir Preferred Stock became entitled to elect two directors to the Board of Directors of Clabir, and effective January 30, 1989, Mr. Maurice A. Halperin and Mr. Barry S. Halperin, who together beneficially own in excess of 70% of the Clabir Preferred Stock, were elected." The Halperins headed Empire of Carolina, a producer of buttons, seasonal decorations, and plastic toys such as Big Wheel.

Despite the problems, Popsicle Canada pushed ahead with the Isaly Klondike Sensation Bar on a stick, and two stickless Sensations were released in the United States. A new ad campaign—the "Famous Mouths"—also debuted with the tag, "No one puts chocolate and ice cream together like Klondike." Four 30-second commercials started with a close-up of a mouth and panned out to reveal Gene Shalit, Vanna White, Steve Allen, or Robin Leach. The campaign was a huge hit, and Henry Clarke even commented, "We could literally run out of product this summer."

A scathing article in *Forbes* that August claimed just that: "Clarke's national ambition for his pet product blinded him to basic business facts. He spent too much money on marketing—some $70 million since 1985." Without the manufacturing to back it up, "every summer, though its three plants are churning out some 56,000 bars an hour, 21 hours a day, seven days a week, the company runs out of product even as its advertising and the weather are revving up demand." It also chastised Clarke for extending the product line, which exacerbated the problem, and it noted that Clabir, for unrelated reasons, had sank into bankruptcy.

Clarke said the "Famous Mouths" campaign was helping: "The first week that those commercials ran, the sales went up, according to Nielsen, 56 percent, which had never happened with a national brand. But that didn't change the fact that we weren't paying the dividends, so this fellow [Halperin] asked to run the company . . . but he had a very different view of what he wanted to do with the company." Further stock purchases gave Empire control of AmBrit, and therefore of Isaly Klondike and its subsidiaries, plus Wilbur Chocolate and Popsicle Canada.

H. William explained, "Now the Halperins immediately said, 'Don't worry, Henry, you can still be CEO of Klondike,' because Henry had loved that so much, and Henry told all of us that's how it was gonna be. And 10 days later, Henry was gone because there was no way Henry Clarke could ever work with a guy like Halperin and take orders from somebody."

Empire cut advertising expenses by one-third, and the "Famous Mouths" received a $200,000 tweaking to show more product.

By 1992, Klondike Lite accounted for 15 percent of sales but ran into some trouble itself. It was advertised as 97 percent fat-free, but the Federal Trade Commission ruled that the claim wasn't true when the coating was considered. The company blamed labeling laws but still took the bar off the market.

Empire, with its toy expertise, introduced a Klondike Ice Cream Parlor in 1992: No pretend Klondikes were included, but kids could make real ice cream. Klondike also ran a "name the Klondike bear contest," with prizes of a trip for two anywhere, a year's supply of Klondikes, and a month's supply. But the winning name was never used, perhaps because the company was sold *again*.

Early in 1993, Empire sold The Isaly Klondike Company and Popsicle Canada to Unilever's Thomas J. Lipton Corporation for $155 million in cash. Henry Clarke was glad to see Unilever expand the business but said that it "cut the quality of the Klondike, and they did another thing which I thought was a bit spiteful, but it's the way big companies operate: They took the Isaly name off the Isaly Klondike." He's pleased, though, that "Unilever, the world's largest ice cream company with unlimited resources, paid us the compliment of running our old [What would you do for a Klondike bar?] commercials." And he added, "I never cease to stop thinking about Klondike, and every time I see one, even though it's someone else's product, if it's not straight in the freezer case, I find myself straightening them."

Both the Hanover and the Rancho Cucamonga plants were closed in favor of nearby Unilever plants. Good Humor executive Dick Newman explained, "It is just a fact of life. When you add new businesses, you can very often get some very real synergies by combining operations. . . . It never should be taken, of course, as a reflection on the people that work there."

Klondike was an adult complement to Unilever's Good Humor business, and Breyer's and Sealtest were acquired a few months later. Unilever also produces Viennetta, Magnum, Popsicle, and licensed novelties such as Reese's ice cream cups and Power Rangers ices. Unilever's newest ice cream acquisition was Ben & Jerry's. A recent study confirms the company's instincts: U.S. sales of ice cream and frozen desserts reached $11.5 billion in 1999, 35 percent of that from novelties. An ACNielsen survey ranks three Klondike products among the top-10-selling ice cream items.

After DDI bought Isaly's stores, they continued to close one by one, often due to third-party leases or changing communities. Jeff Imler was operating the Monroeville, Pennsylvania, Isaly's when he had to close in 1996. He'd worked on and off for Isaly's for almost 30 years. His dad, a 45-year employee, said, "It

Klondikes at Clearwater: Ice cream and air are mixed and frozen at 22 degrees until semisoft, extruded in a square shape and cut by hot wire into bar blocks, put into a cold box (16 minutes at minus 55 degrees, plus fan-induced wind chill), enrobed in a 90-degree chocolate waterfall, run back through the cold box for 30 seconds to harden coating, run past a metal detector, wrapped (foil is cut, crimped, folded, and sealed, as above), grouped in six, have a box formed around them, overwrapped, placed in cases, and put in a freezer for at least 24 hours to reach minus 20 degrees to minimize deterioration. PHOTO BY THE AUTHOR

treated me good. I didn't make a lot of money, but it was gratifying. . . . It was a good family-oriented company. Mr. Isaly cared about us." In fact, he'd sold the Monroeville store to son Jeff, who, he said, "put some money in it and managed it well. The shopping center didn't care whether we put the money in or not, they just closed it up."

Until recently, two Isaly's east of Pittsburgh survived a mile apart at Irwin and Norwin, both opened by Art Lewis, who previously had a bakery in Irwin. Lewis's nephew Paul Sofaly worked at Irwin for 23 years, then ran Norwin for

---

Klondike's Current Parent

The Klondike is just one of thousands of products made by Unilever, a worldwide conglomerate. Its roots stretch back more than a century to British brothers William and James Lever. Their Sunlight detergent was the first packaged, branded laundry soap. The soap was made from vegetable oils, and during World War I, Lever Brothers began applying its oil know-how to margarine. Rival Dutch companies Jurgens and Van den Bergh had earlier pioneered margarine production, and in 1930, all merged to form Unilever. By 1995, Unilever was the world's number-one company ranked by profits, at almost $3 billion. It operates hundreds of companies worldwide. Unilever's product lineup changes as the company is constantly acquiring and divesting.

Some North American food products include Breyer's (including Viennetta) and Sealtest packaged ice cream and frozen yogurt; Good Humor, Popsicle, and licensed novelties such as Reese's ice cream cups and Power Rangers flavored ices; Birds Eye and Gorton's frozen foods; Lipton pastas, soups, and tea (mixes, bags, and bottles); Ragu and Five Brothers pasta sauces; Wishbone dressing; Lawry's and Adolph's seasoning; Imperial, Country Crock, I Can't Believe It's Not Butter!, Shedd's Spread, and Promise margarines; Bertolli olive oils; Boursin cheeses; and SlimFast.

Some personal-care products include Suave, Salon Selectives, and Finesse shampoos; Degree and Sure deodorants; Rave and Aqua Net hair sprays; Brut and Fabergé colognes; Calvin Klein's Escape, Eternity, and Obsession fragrances; Elizabeth Arden and Elizabeth Taylor's Black Pearls and White Diamonds fragrances; Flawless Finish makeup; Chloé; Lever 2000, Dove, Shield, Lifebuoy, and Caress soaps; Snuggle and Final Touch fabric softeners; Wisk, Surf, All, and Rinso detergents; Sun Light dish detergent; Pond's and Vasoline products; Q-tips swabs; Cutex nail and cosmetic products; Signal; and Mentadent, Aim, Close-up, and Pepsodent toothpastes.

The recent acquisition of Bestfoods has added even more product lines, including Hellmann's mayonnaise, Thomas' English muffins, Mazola cooking oil, Boboli pizza crusts, Karo corn syrup, Knorr soups and sauces, NutraBlend soy drinks, Rit color dyes, Mueller's pastas, Skippy peanut butter, and Entenmann's baked goods.

Source: Unilever annual reports.

10 years: "You can go into one of these fast foods, they might have two people, but we prepare all the food down there fresh. . . . You need two people up here, one on ice cream, you need about four on the lunch counter, and that's a big payroll today."

The Irwin location retains its cool late '60s decor. It has had a bakery since 1955: Henry Isaly had forbidden it for the first 10 years, but made the exception for Lewis. That part is managed by Joe Ross, one of two original bakers. In 1988, Art Lewis sold the Isaly's to another nephew, Richard Lewis, and it is now managed by his daughter. They'll make a Skyscraper if you ask, but like some of the other surviving delis, they don't use Isaly's brand chopped ham, claiming its taste differs from the original.

Mohammed Saleem, who had sold his five Isaly's a decade earlier, bought Norwin in 1994. He also bought the Bellevue Sweet William, and his relatives run Homestead and East Ohio Street. But luck and customers were hard to find at Norwin, and it closed in 1997.

Of the hundreds of Isaly's in Ohio, almost all are gone. In Stow, outside Akron, Isaly's succumbed in 1998 when the lease was not renewed and a drugstore replaced it. But two employees opened Isaly's II in the adjacent Colonade Building, incorporating the old booths, stools, and wooden phone booth. The Colonade was actually Isaly's original location: William and Emma Braucher bought it in 1952, then moved it in 1955. Their daughter Sandie later wed clerk John Biltz.

In Youngstown, the Judson Isaly's (named for the cross street) closed in 1997 after 70 years. Don Wissenbach had been operating it since the death of his wife, Wilma, a year earlier. She was assistant manager when they met in 1948, and she bought the store in 1977. "She was always there," said Don, "it was her life." Before her passing, Wilma said the store hadn't changed much, except for one thing: "These stores used to get deliveries two times a day."

Don said that it had become hard to find good workers, a common refrain. John Isaly, who closed his Marion Isaly Shoppe after 25 years, said the same:

The Klondike Lineup

Klondikes now come in 13 flavors: Almond, Candy Bar Swirl, Cappuccino, Caramel Crunch, Chocolate (ice cream), Dark Chocolate, Heath, Krispy Krunch, Neapolitan, Original Vanilla, Reduced Fat/No Sugar Added (vanilla with chocolate coating, but only a four-ounce rather than five-ounce bar), Strawberry Swirl, and York Peppermint Patty.

Klondike has been the best-selling ice cream novelty since at least 1996 (and perhaps as far back as 1989). The Klondike line has blossomed into other novelties, too, including Klondike Choco Taco, Klondike Choc Burger, and three versions each of Klondike Kones and Big Bear sandwiches. The Klondike Krunch, introduced in 1994, is on a stick (the only way they were made in Youngstown for half a century). Movie Bites are sold in theaters.

Are There Still Isaly's?

Yes, a handful of stores survive, but few retain the look of the midcentury delis, and some are simply a deli counter within another business.

3310 Kent Road, Stow, Ohio (no longer an official franchise)
3309 South Avenue, Youngstown, Ohio (no longer an official franchise)
531 Lincoln Avenue, Bellevue, Pennsylvania (also a Sweet William)
Lovedale and Glassport Roads, Elizabeth, Pennsylvania
Route 837, Elrama, Pennsylvania
317 East 8th Avenue, Homestead, Pennsylvania
327 Main Street, Irwin, Pennsylvania
1160 Country Club Drive, Monongahela, Pennsylvania (also the
   Country Club Deli)
147 South Market Street, New Wilmington, Pennsylvania
537 East Ohio Street (north side), Pittsburgh
1649 Perry Highway/Route 19, Portersville, Pennsylvania (no longer
   an official franchise)
Penn Plaza, Turtle Creek, Pennsylvania
2400 Jefferson Street, Washington, Pennsylvania
448 Perrysville Avenue/Route 19, West View, Pennsylvania
3246 Main Street, Weirton, West Virginia

The West View Isaly's retains much of its midcentury ambience. PHOTO BY THE AUTHOR

"The work ethic is just unbelievably different." Bob Sestokas, with Isaly's since 1952, said that he closed his Lawrenceville store in 1996 partly due to poor help.

Bill Gallagher, a manager at King's Family Restaurants in the 1990s, noted, "We think it's gotten worse, but it's just different than our generation. They don't want to be in a 50- or 60-hour-a-week job like their parents, but their technical skills are much better. Back when I started, managers could say, 'It's my way or the highway.' Now they'll choose the highway, because they can go somewhere else."

Just one Isaly's remains in Youngstown, at 3309 South Avenue. Kathy and James Scheetz run the last of three stores her father, Ed Harvischak, bought in 1966. You can get good food and shakes, but it's mostly locals who go there now. "Once grocery stores got their delis," said Kathy, "it killed business in the front end of the store."

The Youngstown plant was bought by U-Haul in 1977, and it's been cleaned up some in recent years. In Marion, the original Isaly's plant sits quietly among weeds, while the 1947 plant was completely remodeled into offices. The former Chief Dairy in Upper Sandusky has produced fruit drinks and flavor powders for the past decade. The Fort Wayne and New Wilmington plants were knocked down years ago, but a homey Isaly's still operates next door to the latter.

The Isaly's in West View, Pennsylvania, is the nearest example of what an old store was like. Tom Weisbecker, a former Sweet William manager, still has

When Mohammed Saleem bought the Norwin Isaly's, he updated it with additions such as the overhead cigarette display to stay competitive. PHOTO BY THE AUTHOR

great food and souvenirs, but he just replaced the Ackerman cabinets with a counter and stools: "The cabinets looked nice, he said, "but it doesn't pay the mortgage, and at night, people head to the soft serve."

In Turtle Creek, Pennsylvania, Darylene and Warren Gwillim have run an Isaly's in a small strip mall since 1996. They serve all the dairy's traditional ice cream flavors along with sandwiches and Frosty Flips, a drink which tastes like a Creamsicle. Anyone wanting to hear some Isaly's history can talk with employee Eleanor Essick, who's worked for the company since 1958.

Some of the remaining Isaly's resemble minimarts, like in Elrama and Elizabeth, Pennsylvania. Jay Deily explained, "Clabir was exploring the idea of gas station and deli." In Portersville, north of Pittsburgh on Route 19, Eppinger's Restaurant is more restaurant and lawn ornament shop, but Dorothy (Eppinger) Curry has had a small Isaly's Quik Shoppe since 1963. The tiny deli and ice cream counter belies Dorothy's wide travels—she's visited 124 countries.

Picturing Isaly's

Isaly's also left its imprint on artists. Kevin Ryan painted the still slowly decaying Braddock Isaly's. 18-by-34-inch watercolor, 1992. KEVIN AND KIM RYAN

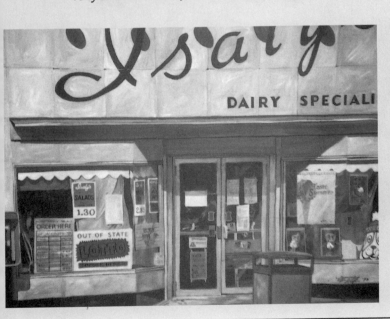

Mary Mazziotti painted this view of the store that sat a block away from her house in Lawrenceville. She said, "My husband has a connection with Isaly's, too. His great-grandparents used to pasture their cows on the land where the Isaly's old headquarters was in Oakland." 24-by-32-inch acrylic on panel, 1993. MARY MAZZIOTTI, COLLECTION OF DON MCKEE

Catherine Q. DeMattia was a regular at the Stow Isaly's and included many real customers and employees in her drawing. 22-by-34-inch pencil, 1997. TOM KNIGHT

Robert Qualters added text over the years to his view of the Boulevard salesroom. 63-by-72-inch oil on canvas. COLLECTION OF OWEN CANTOR FAMILY, PHOTO BY STEPHEN HORNIK

Harold Bricker runs the store in East Liverpool, Ohio, that his dad opened in 1930. Harold said it's been called Bricker's since a 1968 remodeling: "The Isaly Company in my estimation was falling apart at a rapid pace . . . and it was my decision at that time to change our course." A Bricker's in New Brighton, Pennsylvania, has been run by Dorothy Bricker and son Richard Jr. since 1950. Dorothy dropped Isaly's about 1970: "They wanted to deliver milk and ice cream [just] two days a week, curb service."

Isaly's still makes a number of products. Chopped ham and barbecue sauce are easy to find in regional supermarkets and convenience stores. Isaly's ice cream is now made by Reinholds, on Pittsburgh's north side. All the packaging has been updated in red and yellow with a nostalgia theme; Jay Deily said that market studies have found 90 percent name recognition in the region.

Deily likes the traditional Isaly's store, "but I also recognize today's economy and competition, and I think this concept is a viable concept, but it depends on where it's at, and in some ways maybe it needs to become a more upscale type of place, and you seek those areas."

Indicative of the changing commercial landscape is the fate of Isaly's Deli in German Village, a National Register neighborhood in Columbus, Ohio. Though never part of the big Isaly's chain, this Isaly's fit nicely within the district's 1,600 renovated buildings, many dating to the mid-nineteenth century. A 32-room bookstore and locally owned coffee shop sat across the street, but Isaly's lease was not renewed at the close of 2000. Instead, the brick corner building now houses a Starbucks.

• • •

There are now more Isaly's collectors than there are employees. Bill Andrews traces his fondness to a yearly visit to the local Isaly's: "One thing I definitely remember from Isaly's is how different the ice cream tasted com-

Does Isaly's Still Make Products?

You may have seen its chipped ham in stores, but Isaly's still makes other products too. Just ask your grocer whether the store carries Isaly's products.

The Finest **Swiss Cheese** In the World can be Purchased at Isaly's

Chopped ham (bulk and in packages)
Barbecue sauce (original and spicy)
Bologna (Jumbo)
Breast of turkey
Smoked, honey-cured ham
Swiss cheese (bulk and in packages)
American cheese (bulk)
Ice cream (chocolate, cookies in vanilla, French vanilla, Neapolitan, rainbow, strawberry, toasted almond fudge, vanilla, Whitehouse)
Premade sandwiches (sold in convenience stores)

pared to the 'discount' brands from the A&P or Kroger's. It was so rich and creamy. Unfortunately, I also remember that summer day in 1970 when the Isaly company announced they were closing the Youngstown plant for good. Along with the plant closing, they also closed many of the local dairy stores, including the one my family frequented on our yearly visits. My heart sank, knowing a tradition was about to end."

Before his passing in 1997, Art Frank sold his collection. Much of it went to Dave Sinkele, who has amassed a staggering collection of signs, calendars, menu boards, and china. He estimates that Isaly's produced 110 different bottles—he has about 100—but said there are even *more* fervent collectors of Isaliana.

Bob Pierce became a collector when he was moving and discovered his old cap, assistant manager pin, Skyscraper scoop, and a paycheck—his first—for $17.53. Pierce has since re-created an Isaly's counter in his basement with a tin ceiling, tables, and two white Hamilton-Beach milk shake mixers from the Boulevard.

Weirton's Fran Czernek retired from managing in 1987, but she and her husband still collect Isaly's souvenirs. They're looking for a replica truck like ones once sold in the stores; no luck, but they have seen a real one: "on Route 18 on the way to Washington, Pennsylvania . . . but the name 'Isaly's' has faded. How ironic."

George Krohe said that both business and customers have changed so much: "In those days, somebody would come in for a cup of coffee and a hard roll maybe, spend 25¢, and sit at the table, and we would provide them with a clean table and napkins and carry it over on a tray, and after he was through, we'd clean up the table. If somebody came in and the table wasn't clean, they'd have a fit. Now, my God, people go into these convenience stores and buy the stuff and go out and sit on the curb and eat it. . . . The thing for them to have done would have been to say, 'OK, we're gonna go into convenience stores,' [but] it takes guts, and there weren't enough, if you want to call it gamblers, involved to make that move."

Many claim that the third-generation Isalys let things slide, but H. William responded, "All I know is the cousins that were really involved in the business from William R. to John and my brother Tom, myself, we worked long hours, hard hours. There wasn't any fooling around; there weren't lavish parties spending the money. It was work, and we worked very hard. Even though people in general will look back with fond memories of the Isaly's stores, by 1970, the Isaly's store was starting to be an outmoded form of business because we were basically a service store. Everything was done to order. . . . What does convenience mean? It means you don't wait, you just go and pick it up off the shelf. Might not be as good, but boy, you didn't wait around."

Edwin Isaly, a great-nephew of William Isaly, gets emotional thinking about his family's business: "When I look at where my family came from and what they did, the kinds of services they provided, not just selling the product, but the *services* they provided, I feel like we made a worthwhile contribution to the development of this country, very regionally, but we did it. I can look back at the heyday of Isaly's and I can say yes, we did *good* things for people. And I guess that makes me real proud."

APPENDIX A

Isaly Family Tree

THIS TREE SHOWS THE RELATIONSHIPS OF SOME ISALY FAMILY MEMBERS. IT IS not complete, as there were hundreds more descendants, and dozens of those were involved in the company.

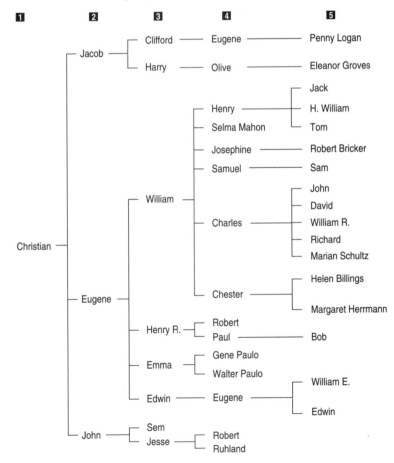

APPENDIX B

Isaly's Plants and Stores

THIS LIST IS CULLED FROM ARTICLES, COMPANY PHONE LISTS, AND, MOST OF ALL, city directories. It is only as good as those sources and may contain errors. Only those years documented are listed. Stores were often in business much longer.

About 615 stores are listed. One trend evidenced is the tendency of Isaly's to move within a block in search of the lowest rent available, so there are really fewer than 615 "locations." Some stores were not part of the company chain.

ISALY'S PLANTS

Main plants

Akron	1680 E. Market St., 1934–50
Canton	2303 Tuscarawas W, 1936–44
	2240 Tuscarawas W, 1945–68
Columbus	2800 N. High, 1936–54
Mansfield	East Temple Court, 1902–09
	7–19 N. Franklin Ave., 1909–67
	12–24 N. Franklin Ave., 1937–61
Marion	226–228 N. Prospect St., 1914–15
	202–206 N. Prospect St., 1915–47
	365 E. Center St., 1947–69
Pittsburgh	3380 Blvd. of the Allies, 1932–78
Youngstown	1033 Mahoning Ave., 1918–70

Related sites

Ft. Wayne, IN	Isaly's Creamery Products, 602 W. Main Street, 1936–59
Marshalltown, IA	Marshall Creamery Co., 119 E. State St., 1945–67
New Wilmington, PA	New Wilm. Cheese Co., Vine St., 1945–70
North Jackson, OH	Isaly Dairy Farm, Akron-Youngstown Rd. at Bailey Rd., c.1920–65
Pittsburgh, PA	Warehouse, 3133 Forbes Ave., ?–1973
Upper Sandusky, OH	Chief Dairy Products Co., 422 W. Guthrie St., 1934–58
Youngstown, OH	Truck garage, 853–855 Mahoning Ave., 1945–65
	Carpenter shop, 1007 Mahoning Ave., 1940–49
	Gas station, 1021 Mahoning Ave., c.1930–70
	Stables, 1544 Mahoning Ave., 1947
	Warehouse, 1589 Mahoning Ave., 1948–49

Recent plants

Evans City, PA	Fort Pitt Brand Meats, W. Main & Pattison Sts., ?–1991
Hanover, PA	Hanover Klondike Co., 877 York St., 1978–93
	Distribution warehouse, 1275 High St., 1989–93
Clearwater, FL	Klondike Southeast, 5400 118th Ave. N, 1982–present
Rancho Cucamonga, CA	Klondike Pacific, 10888 7th St., 1985–93

ISALY'S STORES

Ohio

Akron

Lakemore, 1500 Akron-Canton Rd., 1965–70
#12, 548 S. Arlington, 1939
#7, 1497 Astor Ave., 1939–69
#11, 797 W. Bowery, 1939–65
968 Copley Rd., 1960
#9, 151 E. Cuyahoga Falls Ave., 1939–65
#14, 458 E. Exchange, 1939–66
501 W. Exchange, 1939–60
#19, 1071 W. Exchange St., 1960–70
1167 Grant, 1939
Wooster Hawkins, 1507 S. Hawkins Ave., 1960–69
6 S. Howard, 1930–39
Kenmore, 1008 Kenmore Blvd., 1939–66
164 S. Main, 1939
336 S. Main, 1939
1086 S. Main, 1939–60
#24, 1510 S. Main, 1965–70
Coventry, 3333 Manchester Rd., 1965–70
#8, 599 E. Market St., 1965
#10 salesroom, 1680 E. Market St., 1934–65
#4, 814 W. Market St., 1939–69
#20 Fairlawn, 2725 W. Market St., 1965–69
#6 Goodyear Heights, 314 Pioneer, 1939–96
#15, 458 E. South, 1939–66
Turkeyfoot, 446 Turkeyfoot Lake Rd., 1965–70
#17, 451 Wooster Ave., 1960–66
#13, address unknown, 1966

Alliance
1250 E. State St., 1940–69
Shopping plaza, 1959

Andover
E. Main St. at village square, 1940–55
Address unknown, 1965

Ashland
35 E. Main St., 1940–70
Isaly's Swiss Dairy Store, 417 E. Main St., 1964

Ashtabula
4648 Main St., 1940–65
Saybrook, 2396 W. Prospect Rd., 1965–71

Ashtabula Harbor
525 Lake Ave., 1940–69

Athens
Address unknown, 1942

Austintown
6000 Mahoning Ave. Austintown Plaza, 1953–70
5505 Mahoning Ave., 1940–45, 1951–59

Barberton (Norton Center)
3140 Greenwich Rd., 1965–70
#2, 179 Wooster Rd. N, 1960–70
#3, 1115 Wooster Rd. N, 1965–70

Bellafontaine
114 S. Main St., 1940–70

Bellaire
3348 Belmont St., 1939–70

Bellevue
(Mansfield #30) 117 W. Main St., 1939–70

Boardman
(Boardman Plaza) 263 Boardman-Canfield Rd., 1952–81
Woodworth, 8590 Market St. Ext., 1964–90
5904 South Ave., 1961–86

Bowling Green
104 S. Main St., 1940–77

Bridgeport (1st)
201 Lincoln Ave., 1939–42

Bucyrus
125 S. Sandusky Ave., 1940–66
825 S. Sandusky Ave., 1965–70

Campbell
38 12th St., 1940–67
Wilson Ave. near Center St., dates unknown

Canfield
#1, 24 S. Broad St., 1937–70
Colonial Plaza, 417 E. Main St., 1962–70

Canton
6, 403 Clarendon Ave. NW, 1938–68
1, 1132 Cleveland Ave. NW, 1936–65
S. Canton, 3700 Cleveland Ave. SW, 1960–69
N. Canton, 708 S. Main, 1940–70

7 old, N. Canton, 126 S. Main, 1940–50
5, 1936 Mahoning Rd. NE, 1938–45
9, 2931 Mahoning Rd. NE, 1960–69
2 old, 440 Market Ave. N, 1936–45
7 new, 408 Market Ave. S, 1950–66
4, 1262 Maryland Ave. SW, 1938–66
2 new, 2001 Tuscarawas E, 1960–70
3 (plant), 2303 Tuscarawas W, 1936–68
8, 1107 Tuscarawas W, 1950–65
Meyers Lake Plaza, 1340 Whipple Ave. NW, 1960–70

Carey   116 N. Vance St., 1948–58
Carrolton   100 Public Square, 1940–70
Chagrin Falls   16 Main St., 1965–70
Chardon   111 Main St., 1965
Chillicothe   76 N. Paint St., 1940–52
Circleville   Address unknown, 1940–42
Cleveland   Bedford, 844 Broadway, 1964–69
Berea (Mansfield #15), 77 Front St., 1940–65
Brook Park #1, 6272 Engle Rd., 1964–69
Brook Park #2, 15069 Snow Rd., 1964–69
Garfield Heights, 5727 Turney Rd., 1964–69
Independence, 6531 Brecksville Rd., 1964–69
Maple Heights, 5781 Dunham Rd., 1964–69
Mayfield, 1505 Golden Gate Pl., 1969
Mayfield Heights, 6420 Mayfield Rd., 1965
Parkview, 1830 Snow Rd., 1964–68
Parkview, 6039 State Rd., 1964–68

Clyde   Address unknown, 1940–43
Columbiana   7 S. Main St., 1930s–70
Columbus   3325 E. Broad St., 1950–59
1341 W. Broad St., 1945–50
2395 W. Broad St., 1936–59
1097 Cleveland Ave., 1945
2503 Cleveland Ave., 1940–53
Isaly Shoppe, 2001 E. Dublin Granville Rd., 1979
267 W. 11th Ave., 1950
1238 W. Fifth Ave., 1950–53
1790 W. Fifth Ave., 1950
1559 N. 4th St., 1950–53
Graceland Shopping Center, 79 Graceland Blvd., 1959–69
Grandview, 1299 Grandview Ave., 1945–53
Grandview, 1305 Grandview Ave., 1940
Great Eastern Shopping Center, 860 S. Hamilton Rd., 1966–69
Central Point Shopping Center, 632 Harrisburg Pike, 1966–69
155 N. High St., 1945–53
579 N. High St., 1940–53
1205 N. High St., 1936–66
1620 N. High St., 1940–53
University, 1864 N. High St., 1940–69
2800 N. High St., 1936–53
3397 N. High St., 1945–59
Great Southern Shopping Center, 3879 S. High St., 1959–70
2997 Indianola Ave., 1950–53
#31 Lane Ave. Shopping Center, 1609 W. Lane Ave., 1953–66
590 E. Livingston Ave., 1940–53
1035 E. Livingston Ave., 1942–53
176 E. Main St., 1940–50
1436 E. Main St., 1945–69
1953 S. Mallway, 1950
1021 Mt. Vernon Ave., 1945
1666 Neil Ave., 1945–53
2109 Neil Ave., 1950
Great Western Shopping Center, 3384 North Blvd., 1965–70

Columbus (continued)

1255 Oak St., 1940–53
University City Shopping Center, 2869 Olentangy
    River Rd., 1965–69
67 Parsons Ave., 1950–53
968 Parsons Ave., 1945–59
1884 Parsons Ave., 1936–59
49 E. State St., 1940–59
1436 Sullivant Ave., 1950–53
2524 Sullivant Ave., 1945–50
464 Vermont Place, 1953
2692 Westerville Rd., 1950–59
1030 E. Whittier, 1950
1048 E. Whittier, 1945
Berwick Plaza Shopping Center, 2801 Winchester Pike, 1966–69
Arthur & Bertha Isaly deli, 13 Central Market, 1936
Arthur H. Isaly cheese, 548 Mohawk, 1945
Arthur Isaly deli, 9 Central Market, 1950–53

165 S. 4th St., 1950–53
Carl M. Isaly cheese, 765 S. 3rd St., 1945
Carl M. & Son (Richard A.), 765 S. 3rd St., 1950–53
23 Central Market, 1953–59
Chas. W. & Son deli, 10 Central Market, 1936
H.R. & Son (Paul H.), 31 Central Market, 1936
48 N. Market, 1936
H.R. Isaly, 5 N. Market House, 1945–53
H.R.I. Sons (Paul & Leroy), 31 Central Market, 1950–65
H.R. Isaly Sons Deli, 650 S. 3rd St., 1965–00
H.R. Isaly & Sons, 6072 Busch Blvd., 1979
Isaly Bros. (Carl & Arthur), 23 Central Market, 1936
765 S. 3rd St., 1936
Isaly Bros. (Carl & Richard A.), 23 Central Market, 1950

Cortland   238 W. Main St., 1940–70
Coshocton   (Mansfield #18) 432 Main St., 1940–69
Cuyahoga Falls   #1, 2157 Front, 1939–66
                     #5, 3245 Oakwood Dr., 1960–70
                     #2, 1674 State Rd., 1965–70
                     #3, 2220 State Rd., 1960
                     #4, 2731 State Rd., 1960–70

Damascus   Address unknown, 1940–70
Deforest   Address unknown, dates unknown
Delaware   Address unknown, 1940–43
East Liverpool   116 E. 6th St., 1930–68
East Palestine   77 N. Market St., 1932–70s
East Rochester   Probably Lincoln Highway, 1970
Ellet   Address unknown, 1940
Elyria   (Mansfield #7), 346 Broad St., 1937–66
                     (Mansfield #11), 529 Broad St., 1937–60
                     360 Cleveland, 1949–65
Findlay   Address unknown, 1940–43
Fostoria   Address unknown, 1940–43
Fremont   Address unknown, 1940–43
                     Potter Village Shopping Center, 1138 Oak Harbor Rd., 1959–70
Galion   118 Harding Way E, 1938–69
Geneva   11 W. Main St., 1940–65
Girard   1 N. State, 1932–42
                     #1, 2 N. State, 1943–70
                     #2, 716 N. State, 1939–65
Hartville   S. Prospect St., 1940–65
Hubbard   29 N. Main St., 1940–70
Hudson   190 N. Main St., 1940–69
Jefferson   N. Chestnut Ave., 1940–65
Kent   116 S. Water, 1932–57
                     University Plaza, 156 Cherry, 1959–70

Kenton	23 Detroit St., 1940–70
Kinsman	Address unknown, 1940–70
Lake Milton	Rt. 18, 1940–65
Lancaster	160 W. Main St., 1936–50
Leetonia	254 Main St., 1940–70
Lima	56 Public Square, 1938–46
	800 W. North St., 1949–52
	976 St. Johns Ave., 1950–52
Lisbon	125 S. Market St., 1940–50
	113 S. Market St., 1951–82
Lodi	(Mansfield #25) 1940–47
Logan	Address unknown, 1942
London	19 S. Main St., 1940–53
Lorain	(Mansfield #8, #16, #17)
	632 Broadway, 1937
	73 Pearl Ave., 1937
Loudonville	(Mansfield #29) 1940–47
Louisville	117 E. Main, 1940–70
Lowellville	135 E. Water St., 1931–72
Madison	10 W. Main St., 1965–69
Malvern	Reed Ave. & Grant St., 1965
Mansfield	846 Ashland Rd., 1957–63
	Isaly's Swiss Dairy Store, 1965–67
	Isaly's Swiss Dairy Store, 398 S. Diamond St., 1963–67
	#6, 60 W. 4th, 1917–39, 1961–70
	58 W. 4th, 1941–59
	#10, 15–21 N. Franklin Ave. (salesroom), 1937–61
	#19, 343 Lexington Ave., 1943–70
	5 N. Main: Richland Trust, 1930–34
	80 N. Main, 1936–39
	88 N. Main, 1941–49
	305 Marion Ave., 1937–57
	Isaly's Swiss Dairy Store, 1963–67
	#5, 56 Park Ave. W, 1924–26
	46 Park Ave. W, 1936–51
	50 Park Ave. W, 1955–63
	Mansfield Square Shopping Center, 1230 Park Ave. W, 1965–70
	461 Spring Mill, 1926–37
Marion	City market, 1920
	Salesroom, 365 E. Center, 1943–70
	766/8 Davids, 1925–27
	128 S. Main, 1925–36
	151 S. Main, 1945–66
	216 N. Prospect, 1950–62
	Isaly Shoppe, 1081 Mt. Vernon Ave., 1968–96
Martins Ferry	36 S. Fourth St., 1946–93
Marysville	113 E. Fifth, 1940–66
Massillon	27 Lincoln Way E, 1940–50s
	#2 Town Plaza, 248 Federal Ave. NW, 1960–70
Masury	Elm & Miller Sts., 1940–70
McDonald	Address unknown, 1940
Medina	(Mansfield #13) 4 Public Square, 1940–48
	Medina Plaza Shopping Center, Rt. 42, 907 N. Court St., 1959–70
Mentor	7323 Lakeshore Blvd., 1965–69
Millersburg	(Mansfield #12) 1947
Mineral Ridge	211 Main St., 1940–66
Minerva	204 N. Market St., 1940–70
Mingo Junction	631 Commercial St., 1932–78
Mogadore	10 S. Cleveland Ave., 1965
Mt. Gilead	W. High St., 1940–56
Mt. Union	Address unknown, 1940
Mt. Vernon	(Mansfield #28) 109 S. Main St., 1935–54
New Middletown	204 Sycamore Dr., 1965–70

New Philadelphia	149 N. Broadway, 1965
New Waterford	Address unknown, 1940
Newark	45 N. 3rd St. at W. Church St., 1948–53
	569 Hebron, Southgate Shopping Center, 1966–69
Newton Falls	26 Broad St., 1940–65
Niles	7 S. Main, 1932–67
	301 Robbins Ave., 1940–42
	416 Robbins Ave., 1943–67
	402 Eastwood Mall, Rt. 422, 1970
North Baltimore	121 Main St., 1941
North Jackson	10946 Mahoning Ave. Ext., 1965–79
	106 N. Salem-Warren Rd., 1980–86
North Lima	Main St., 1940–50
	South Ave. Ext., 1951–62
Norwalk	(Mansfield #26) 54 E. Main St., 1932–64
Oberlin	(Mansfield #1) 9 W. College St., 1935–61
Orwell	Address unknown, 1940
Painesville	187 Main St., 1940s–65
Parma	#1, 1830 Snow Rd., 1965–69
	#2, State Rd. & Maplecrest, 1965–69
Piqua	Address unknown, 1940–43
Poland	204 S. Main St., 1933–86
Randolph	Address unknown, 1965–70
Ravenna	125 E. Main St., 1940–70
	946 E. Main St., 1965
Salem	241 E. State St., 1940–67
	496 E. State St., 1932–40
Sandusky	(Mansfield #14) 147 Columbus Ave., 1937–66
Sebring	280 15th St., 1940–70
Shelby	57 W. Main St., 1935–71
	83 Wall St., 1929–37
Sidney	114 N. Main St., 1940–66
Solon	33587 Aurora Rd., 1964–69
Springfield	2023 Lagonda Ave., 1940
	38 S. Limestone St., 1939–47
	59–61 W. Main St., 1939–52
	"Cream station," 327 W. Main St., 1936
	516 E. Pleasant, 1940
	119 E. Ward, 1940
	644 S. Yellow Springs, 1940
Steubenville	147 N. 4th, 1948–78
	159 N. 4th, 1932–48
Stow	3390 Kent Rd., 1929–55
	3322 Kent Rd., 1955–98
	Isaly's II, 3310 Kent Rd., 1998–present
Streetsboro	9083 State Rd., Rt. 14, 1959–69
Struthers	Old #1, 119 S. Bridge St., 1925–31
	New #1, 123 S. Bridge St., 1931–70
	#2, 563 Fifth St., 1946–70
	Struthers Plaza, 1014 Fifth St., 1962–88
Tallmadge	37 Midway Plaza, Brittain Rd., 1960–70
Tiffin	688 W. Market, Westgate Shopping Center, 1940–70
Toronto	221 N. 4th St., 1933–70
Troy	13 S. Market St., 1940–66
Upper Sandusky	113 N. Sandusky, 1959–62
Urbana	Address unknown, 1940–43
Vermilion	Address unknown, 1940
Wadsworth	117 Main St., 1965–70
Wapakoneta	Address unknown, 1940–43
Warren	#8, 2067 Elm Rd. Ext., 1965–70
	#6, 185 High St. NE, 1965–69
	#3, 404 Market St., 1965–70
	#1, 804 W. Market St., 1932–95

#7, 2710 Montclair Ave., 1965
#2, 1105 Park Ave., 1965–70
#9, 1809 Parkman Rd., 1965
Trumbull, 111 Trumbull Plaza, Parkman Rd. Ext., 1965–70
#4, 2681 Youngstown Rd., 1965–69

Washington Court House	203 Court St., 1940–42
Waynesburg	N. Main & Lisbon Sts., 1940–70
Wellington	(Mansfield #27) 1941–47
Wellsville	451 Main St., 1933–70
Westerville	30 N. State St., 1940–69
Wickliffe	30330 Euclid Ave., 1965–70
Willard	Address unknown, 1940
Willoughby	9231 Chillicothe Rd., 1965–69
Willowick	32600 Vine St., 1965–69
Wooster	152 E. Liberty St., 1952–54
	203 W. Liberty St., 1954–70
Worthington	673 High St., 1953
Xenia	40 S. Detroit St., 1940–50
Youngstown	1029 Albert St., 1931

1526 Belmont Ave., 1923–69
2929 Belmont Ave., 1956–57
3135 Belmont Ave., 1958–70
Cornersburg, 3381 Canfield Rd., 1956–82
11 Central Square, 1924
39 Central Square, 1925–69
318 Covington St., 1931–65
1365 Elm St., 1927–69
236 E. Federal St., 1955–67
265 E. Federal St., 1926–35
277 E. Federal St., 1937–44
257 W. Federal St., 1924–85
1510 W. Federal St., 1927–37
1514 W. Federal St., 1938–60
Fifth Ave., 1947
900 Foster St., 1961–69
McGuffey Plaza, 769 N. Garland Ave., 1954–70
316 Girard-Hubbard Rd., 1952–53
397 Girard-Hubbard Rd., 1965–66
901 Glenwood Ave., 1948–70
Glenwood, 2640 Glenwood Ave., 1927–34, 1964–77
602 Hillman St., 1931–32
Hillman, 1902 Hillman St., 1934–67
1365 Himrod Ave., 1933–70
1818 Hubbard Rd., 1950–58
1407 E. Indianola Ave., 1965
2242 Logan Ave., 1925–46
407 Madison Ave., 1931–64
Salesroom, 1033 Mahoning Ave., 1965–70
Steel St., 1650 Mahoning Ave., 1937–49, 1954–70
2523 Mahoning Ave., 1948–58
2600 Mahoning Ave., 1960–76
Wickliffe, 4186 Mahoning Ave., 1949–76
544 Market St., 1940
1406 Market St., 1923–31
1408 Market St., 1932–45
1513 Market St., 1946–69
2012 Market St., 1931–48
Indianola, 2624 Market St., 1924–30, 1951–69
Indianola, 2633 Market St., 1931–33
Indianola, 2706 Market St., 1933–50
Judson, 3632 Market St., 1927–97
Lincoln Knolls Plaza, 2916 McCartney Rd., 1957–81
Midlothian, 1948 E. Midlothian, 1928–72

Youngstown (continued)

Mill Creek Park, 1969
927 North Ave., 1956–60
901 Oak St., 1949–54
907 Oak St., 1965–69
2003 Ohio Ave., 1931–68
1287 Poland Ave., 1950–59
Wedgewood Plaza, 1725 S. Raccoon Rd., 1962–67
Isaly Shoppe, 1967–71
E. Rayen Ave., 1963
200 W. Rayen Ave., 1940–62
Rt. 90, 1958
1235 St. Clair Ave., 1931–42
Mill Creek, 1260 S. Schenley Ave., 1965–70
Shields Rd., 1958
1323 South Ave., 1929–49, 1961–62
1339 South Ave., 1932–33
3309 South Ave., 1936–present
Mathews Rd., 5904 South Ave., 1965–70
5136 Southern Blvd., 1931–34
5234 Southern Blvd., 1965
2 N. State, 1967
4 Sycamore Dr., 1961–62
Wedgewood Plaza, Raccoon Rd., 1962
1077 Wick Ave., 1931–67
1757 Wilson Ave., 1931
Youngstown-Akron Rd., 1955–64
Isaly Shoppe, 131 Lincoln Ave., 1967–70

Pennsylvania

Aliquippa	#1, 522 Franklin Ave., 1930–70
	1192 Main St.-Maratta Rd., 1960
	#2, 1134 Main St., 1965–70
Ambridge	#1, 643 Merchant St., 1932–80
	#2, 1302 Duss Ave., c.1950–65
Baden	Northern Lights Shoppers City, c.1950–70
	3798 Duss Ave., 1965–70
Beaver	610 3rd St., 1964–70
Beaver Falls	#1, 1310 7th Ave., 1927–70
	College Hill, 32nd St. & 4th Ave., 1952
Bellevue	(New) 531 Lincoln Ave. (Shoppe at 516), 1934–80
	(Old) 557 Lincoln Ave., 1932–34
Bessemer	11 E. Poland Ave., 1940–70
Bethel Park	Country Gdn., 5190 Library Rd., 1940–80
	South Hills Village, Rt. 19 S, 1965–80
Blairsville	104 E. Market St., 1952–70
Braddock	(New) 734 Braddock Ave., 1940–87
	(Old) 740 Braddock Ave., 1931–40
Bridgeville	500 Washington Ave., 1951–56
	Great Southern Shopping Center, Washington Pike, 1955–78
Brownsville	24 Market St., dates unknown
Butler	#4, Bon Aire Shopping Center, 1965–70
	#2, 359 Center St., 1940–66
	#3, 306 N. Main St., 1944–78
	109 S. Main St., 1936–46
	#1, 118 Point Plaza, Rt. 11, 1965–82
	Greater Butler Shopping Mart, Rt. 8 S, 1965–82
Byersdale	3798 Duss Ave., 1953–91
Canonsburg	24 Pike St., 1938–56
	Donaldson Crossroads Shopping Center, 1965–87
Carnegie	15 W. Main St., 1933–80
Charleroi	524 Fallowfield Ave., 1932–82
Clairton	564 Miller Ave., 1940–80

Cochranton	Address unknown, 1940–70
Conneaut Lake	132 Water St., 1951–72
Conway	1241 2nd Ave., 1950s–65
Coraopolis	(New) 423 Mill St., 1946–82
	(Old) 417 Mill St., 1936–46
Darlington	2nd & Market, 1920s–65
Donora	563 McKean Ave., 1935–70
Duquesne	33 W. Grant St., 1933–60
	302 W. Grant Ave., 1965–67
	Duquesne Plaza, 1970–80
East Pittsburgh	824 Linden Ave., 1936–65
Elizabeth	Lovedale & Glassport Rds., 1970s–present
Ellwood City	502 Lawrence Ave., 1940–70
Elrama	Rt. 837, 1982–present
Etna	358 Butler St., 1933–80
Evans City	229 E. Main St., 1937–77
Farrell	#1, 407 Idaho St., 1940–65
	#2, 701 Union St., 1950–80
Fox Chapel	Freeport Rd., Aspinwall, 1956–82
Franklin	1233 Liberty St., 1932–70
Freedom	640 3rd Ave., 1940–50
	624 3rd Ave., 1965
Greensburg	21 N. Main St., 1932–81
	2240 Greengate Mall, Rt. 30, 1970–73
Greenville	212 Main St., 1929–77
Grove City	228 S. Broad St., 1940–73
Harrisburg	Capitol Complex, 1982
Hazelwood	4838/40 Second Ave., 1934–67
Homestead	209 E. 8th Ave., 1931–60
	317 E. 8th Ave., 1934–present
Irwin	327 Main St., 1945–present
Jamestown	Main & Liberty Sts., 1930s–70
Jeanette	501 Clay Ave., 1932–78
Johnstown	Richland Mall, 1975–78
Kennedy Township	Kenmawr Shopping Center, 1970–82
Kittanning	128 Market St., 1947–56
Latrobe	903 Ligonier St., 1950–56
Linesville	412 Erie St., 1930s–65
	144 Erie St., 1970–96
Mahoningtown	114 N. Liberty St., 1940–70
McKees Rocks	527 Chartiers Ave., 1934–60
McKeesport	211/15 Fifth Ave., 1968–70 (in The Canopy)
	214 Fifth Ave., 1931–66
	506 Fifth Ave., 1933–70
	1500/2 Lincoln Way, 1942–84
	1607 Evans Ave., 1935–80
	Olympia Shopping Center, Walnut St., 1965–80
Meadville	#1, 253 Chestnut St., 1932–70
	#2, 376 North St., 1949–98
Mercer	118 N. Pitt St., 1940–71
Midland	732 Midland Ave., 1932–69
Millvale	215 North Ave., 1938–87
Monaca	1032 Pennsylvania Ave., 1940–70
Monessen	509 Donner Ave., 1934–85
Monongahela	425 (or 245) Main St., 1934–78
	1160 Country Club Dr., ?–present
Monroeville (2nd)	Miracle Mile Shopping Center, 1954–96
Murrysville	Old William Penn Hwy., 1981
Natrona Heights	Heights Plaza Shopping Center, 1955–87
New Brighton	901 3rd Ave., 1938–60
	1312 7th Ave., 1938
	301 8th St., 1960–70
New Castle	#7, 1028 Croton Ave., 1965–70

New Castle (continued)

#5, 1700 N. Highland Ave., 1941–70
114 N. Liberty, 1941–65
6 N. Mill, 1975
#2, 1225 S. Mill, 1926–70
Westgate, 2028 W. State St., 1965–75
3 E. Washington St., 1935–56
#3, 201 E. Washington St., Corner Mill, 1930–70
351 E. Washington St., 1926–49
2650 E. Washington St., 1965–75
#6, 410 W. Washington St., 1949–65
Calls Plaza, 1710 Wilmington Ave., 1965–75
Lawrence Village, 2703 Ellwood City Rd., 1965–78

New Kensington

971 Fifth Ave., 1931–80
Hillcrest Shopping Center, 143 Leechburg Rd., 1965–80

New Wilmington
North Huntingdon
North Versailles

147 S. Market, 1940–present
Norwin Plaza (now Norwin Towne Square), Rt. 30, 1959–97
16 Rt. 30 Plaza, Rt. 30, 1965–75
Great Valley Shopping Center, Rt. 30, 1960–80

Oil City

#1, 217 Seneca St., 1932–82
#2, 14 E. First St., 1952–70

Pittsburgh

Allison Park, Glannon Shopping Center,
    2412 Ferguson Rd., 1965–80
Allison Park, Hampton Plaza Shopping Center, 1965
Beechview (1st), 1544 Beechview Ave., 1935–47
Beverly Rd. (new), 303 Beverly Rd., 1941–80
Beverly Rd. (old), 313 Beverly Rd., 1932–41
Bigelow Blvd. (2nd), 511 Sixth Ave., 1953–60
Bloomfield, 4748 Liberty Ave., 1936–80
Brookline, 930 Brookline Blvd., 1937–91
Brownsville Plaza, 1100 Brownsville Rd., 1967–78
Butler St., Lawrenceville (new), 4209 Butler St., 1950–96
Butler St. (old), 4211 Butler St., 1932–50
Carrick, 2608 Brownsville Rd., 1934–97
Carrick, Mt. Oliver Plaza, 1965–80
Crafton Ingram Shopping Center, 88 W. Steuben St., 1967–80
Dormont, 2904 W. Liberty Ave., 1931–80
Dormont Junction (2nd), 3261 W. Liberty Ave., 1947–80
Downtown (1st), 423 Fifth Ave., 1939–49
Downtown, 439 Wood St., 1935–89
East End (new), 5813 Penn Ave., 1947–60
East End (old), 5927 Penn Ave., 1937–47
East Hills, East Hills Shopping Center, 1960–77
East Liberty, 6119/25 Penn Ave., 1932–89
East Ohio St., 855 East Ohio St., 1936–67
East Ohio St., 537 East Ohio St., 1933–present
Federal St., 812 Federal St., 1933–60
Federal St. (new), 508 Federal St., 1937–56
Federal St. (old), 500 Federal St., 1934–37
Greentree, 970 Greentree Rd., 1970–80
Greentree Deli, 962 Greentree Rd., 1978–80
Hilltop, 827 Warrington Ave., 1942–60
Homewood (new), 625 N. Homewood Ave., 1938–67
Homewood (old), 619 N. Homewood Ave., 1931–38
Liberty Ave., 627 Liberty Ave., 1935–60
Manchester, 1724 Beaver Ave., 1934–65
Manchester, 1705 Beaver Ave., Chateau Plaza, 1965–75
Mt. Lebanon, 700 Washington Rd., 1931–80
Mt. Lebanon, St. Clair Shopping Center, N. Wren Dr., 1975–80
Mt. Oliver, 230 Brownsville Rd., 1935–80
Murray Ave. (1st), 2032 Murray Ave., 1932–42
Murray Ave., 1940 Murray Ave. (combo Sweet William), 1977–80
North Hills, 4801 McKnight Rd. (N. Hills Village), 1960–80

Pittsburgh (continued)	North Hills, 1008 Northway Mall, 1962–80
	North Side, Allegheny Center Mall (Isaly Shoppe '69), 1967–90
	Oakland, 3714 Forbes Ave., 1933–70
	Penn Ave., 528 Penn Ave., 1940–60
	Penn Hills, 11616 Keleket Dr., Penn Hills Shopping Center, 1975–80
	Perrysville, 3906 Perrysville Ave., 1938–89
	Regent Square, 1115 S. Braddock Ave., 1932–80
	Salesroom, 3380 Blvd. of the Allies, 1931–87
	Shadyside (new), 5502 Walnut St., 1948–70
	Shadyside (old), 5500 Walnut St., 1935–48
	Smithfield St. (1st), 627 Smithfield St., 1938–47
	Smithfield St. (2nd), 635/7 Smithfield St., 1946–67
	South Side, 1715 E. Carson St., 1937–89
	South Side (new), 1302 E. Carson St., 1942–65
	South Side (old), 1500 E. Carson St., 1932–42
	Squirrel Hill, 5808 Forbes Ave., 1931–82
	Stanton Heights, 5347 Mossfield St., 1967–75
	Troy Hill (1st), 1733 Lowrie St., 1941–45
	Uptown (1st), 1319 Fifth Ave., 1935–42
	Virginia Manor, Cochran Rd. at Greentree Rd., 1967–80
	Washington Plaza, Washington Plaza Shopping Center, 1970–78
	West End (new), 443 S. Main St., 1946–67
	West End (old), 403 S. Main St., 1937–46
	Whitehall (later Sweet William), Caste Village, 1975–80
	Wilkinsburg, 766 Penn Ave., 1936–80
	Wilkinsburg, 915/17 Wood St., 1931–70
	Wilkinsburg, 902 Wood St., 1978–99
Pleasant Hills	Grant City/Gold Circle, Curry Hollow Rd., 1975–87
	Southland Shopping Center, Rt. 51, 1960–78
Portersville	1649 Perry Hwy., Rt. 19, Quik Shoppe, 1965–present
Rochester	146 Brighton Ave., 1931–47
	194 Brighton Ave., 1964–70
Sandy Lake	Address unknown, 1940–70
Sewickley	422 Beaver Ave., 1932–84
Sharline	Address unknown, dates unknown
Sharon	37 Chestnut St., 1981
	302 W. Main, 1963
	Hickory Plaza, 2341 Sharon-Mercer Rd., E. State St., 1963–73
	#2, 514 N. Sharpsville Ave., 1939–65
	#3, 721 E. State St., 1939–70
	114 E. State St., 1960
	#1, 49 W. State St., 1939–70
Sharpsburg	(New) 904 Main St., 1948–60
	(Old) 705 Main St., 1934–48
Sharpsville	302 Main St., 1940–65
Slippery Rock	142 S. Main, 1940–70
Swissvale	(2nd) 7542 Dickson St., 1952–75
Tarentum	302 Corbet St., 1946–87
Titusville	112 Spring St., 1940–70
Turtle Creek	522 Penn Ave., 1937–75
	Penn Plaza Shopping Center, 1990–present
Vandergrift	149 Grant Ave., 1947–97
Wampum	Main St., 1940–70
Washington	31 W. Main St., 1932–56
	86 W. Main St., 1970
	2400 Jefferson Ave., 1990–present
	Washington Plaza, 1978
Waynesburg	52–54 W. High St., 1947–70
West Middlesex	222 N. Main St., 1940–70
West Mifflin	Duquesne Village Shopping Center, 1961–80, 1982–c.85
West View	448 Perrysville Rd., 1950–present

Wheatland	66/70 Broadway St., 1960–73
Wilmerding	415 Station St., 1936–80
Zelienople	111 S. Main St., 1940–79

West Virginia
Elm Grove	2085 National Rd., 1947–70
Moundsville	284 Jefferson Ave., 1949–60s
Weirton	(1st) 3246 Main St. (Holidays Cove), 1939–present
Wheeling	1301 Market St., 1939–70

SWEET WILLIAMS
New York
| Brooklyn | King's Hwy. at E 13 & 14 Sts., 1978 |

Ohio
| Steubenville | Fort Steuben Mall, 1974–78 |
| Warren | Eastwood Mall, Rt. 422, 1969–78 |

Pennsylvania
Bellevue	531 Lincoln Ave., 1977–present
Camp Hill	Capital City Mall, 1978
Forest Hills	2020 Ardmore Blvd., 1977–82
Greensburg	Greengate Mall, Rt. 30, 1978–82
	Westmoreland Mall, Rt. 30, 1978
Johnstown	Richland Mall, 1978
Monaca	Beaver Valley Mall, 1970–85
Monroeville	Monroeville Mall, Rt. 22, 1969–87
North Versailles	Eastland Mall, 1978
Penn Hills	Penn Hills Shopping Center, Rodi Rd., 1977–82
Pine Creek	9805 McKnight Rd., 1976–85
Pittsburgh	Downtown, Fifth & Liberty Aves., 1977–85
	Downtown, 808 Liberty Ave., 1977–82
	East Hills, East Hills Shopping Center, 1977
	Greentree, 970 Greentree Rd. (Shoppe in '67), 1977–85
	North Hills, North Hills Village (combo with deli), 1976–87
	North Side, Allegheny Center Mall, 1977–85
	Oakland, 3714 Forbes Ave., 1977–78
	Squirrel Hill, 1940 Murray Ave., 1977–80
	Virginia Manor, Cochran Rd. at Greentree Rd., 1977–80
	Whitehall, Caste Village, 1977–82
Pleasant Hills	Southland Shopping Center, Rt. 51, 1977–80
Reading	4365 Perkiomen Ave., 1978
Sharon	Shenango Mall, 1975–78
State College	Nittany Mall, 1978
Uniontown	1362 W. Main St., 1978
Wyomissing	Berkshire Mall, 1978

West Virginia
| Fairmont | Middletown Mall, 1978–93 |
| Morgantown | Mountaineer Mall, 1978 |

FOR MORE INFORMATION

The Iseli Family World Wide Web Site, www.iseli.org/en, offers a thorough and interesting genealogy of the many family branches.

Isaly's has a website at www.isalys.com, and the Klondike site is www.icecreamusa.com/klondike.

A number of related documents and photos are available at the Historical Society of Western Pennsylvania Library and Archives, 1212 Smallman Street, Pittsburgh, PA 15222-4200, (412) 454-6364, www.pghhistory.org, and the Mahoning Valley Historical Society, 648 Wick Avenue, Youngstown, OH 44502-1289, (330) 743-2589. Both organizations are interested in adding to their collections.

The Architecture Archives at Carnegie Mellon University holds more than 150 architect's drawings of various Isaly company projects. For more information, contact archivist Martin Aurand, 4825 Frew Street, Pittsburgh, PA 15213-3890. A brief description can be found at www.library.cmu.edu./libraries/archarch/isaly.html.

For those interested in ice cream history and memorabilia, contact Ice Screamers, P.O. Box 465, Warrington, PA 18976. A $20 subscription (U.S.) brings four issues of the quarterly newsletter.

The Society for Commercial Archeology is the oldest national organization devoted to the commercial-built environment. Through publications, conferences, and tours, SCA helps preserve, document, and celebrate the structures, highways, and architecture of the twentieth century. Individual membership is $25; family and institutional, $40. SCA, c/o Department of Popular Culture, Bowling Green State University, Bowling Green, OH 43403, www.sca-roadside.org.

For a list of sources referenced for this book, Isaly's recipes, and more illustrations, go to http://bbutko.tripod.com/isaly.html.

ABOUT THE AUTHOR

*B*RIAN BUTKO HAS AN M.A. IN HISTORY FROM DUQUESNE
University in Pittsburgh. He lives in Pittsburgh with his wife
and three children and is author of *The Lincoln Highway*,
coauthor of *Diners of Pennsylvania*, and editor of *Western Pennsylvania
History* magazine. Butko recently directed and mounted an exhibit
on Isaly's that opened at the Senator John Heinz Pittsburgh Regional
History Center.